Praise for A N

"*A New Dawn Awaits* serves as a mirror to each individual's soul potential, as well as a reminder of who we are and where we are heading together in this journey of life. It is profound – a must read for all who want to take part in the positive re-shaping of our planet and our consciousness, into what Eckhart Tolle calls a 'New Earth'."

~ *LINA NAHHAS, Founder, 1-Urban Humanity for the Middle East*

"A panacea for the troubled heart, E.Dee Conrad's *A New Dawn Awaits* speaks the simple and all-embracing message that kindness, compassion and love are the keys to unlocking our own 'Heaven on Earth'."

~ *LYNN SERAFINN, Author of spirituality bestseller* The Garden of the Soul: lessons from four flowers that unearth the Self

"*A New Dawn Awaits* is a book that will help transform the consciousness of humanity. This book is amazing – once I started reading it, I could not put it down. As I read it, the truth about humanity's path became clearer and clearer. I am certain that any reader who is looking for answers to age-old questions will find this book fascinating. While the information is obviously from a higher source, E.Dee does a wonderful job of bringing this message to us in words we can all understand."

~ *DR. PARVIZ RASHVAND, N.D., Doctor of Naturopathic Medicine*

"If you are comfortable with the science and the concepts put forth in the works of authors such as Gregg Braden and Lynne McTaggert, you will love *A New Dawn Awaits*. For Conrad, the basic premise is that our thoughts create our reality and that the power of the human mind is unlimited. Her book shows us how we can all work together to harness this power and create a truly magnificent new world."

~ *MARK KARLSSON, Spiritual and life empowerment coach*

"This book couldn't have come out at a better time – *A New Dawn Awaits* is full of messages that we need to hear, and we need to hear them now. My own near-death experience woke me up to many of the truths contained within this book, so I am fully aware of the importance of sharing such information. E.Dee Conrad shares the messages in a very readable and easy to understand manner. What struck me about her book was that its transformational messages were written in a very down to earth manner. A valuable read for anyone seeking to understand the direction humanity is now heading towards.

~ *ANITA MOORJANI, Near death experiencer,* www.anitamoorjani.com

"In *A New Dawn Awaits*, E.Dee Conrad sees troubled times ahead and provides spiritual guidance on how to deal with these new challenges. Not everyone will agree with her predictions, but no reader can fail to be taken with the elegance of her words and the fluency of the ideas. Written with compassion at its core, this channeled work is truly a poem from the universe – one which speaks to all who are looking for a new way of being."

~ *SAADIA KHAIRI, Financier*

A NEW DAWN AWAITS

The Times Ahead and
How To Shift Your Consciousness

E.Dee Conrad

Blog: http://edeeconrad.com
Twitter: http://twitter.com/edeeconrad
Facebook: http://facebook.com/edee.conrad

A Bright Pen Book

Copyright E.Dee Conrad ©2010

Cover design by Sugarcube Studios

ISBN 978 0 7552 1232 3

Authors OnLine Ltd
19 The Cinques
Gamlingay, Sandy
Bedfordshire SG19 3NU
England

Bright Pen

This book is also available in e-book format, details of which are available at www.authorsonline.co.uk

Lovingly dedicated to my mother, Cheryl Conrad,
who lived this book long before it was written.

Contents

Exercises

Author's Note

In early 2007, I began to have a feeling that I would write a book. At first, I just laughed it off because I, for one, had never had the desire to write a book. As the feeling persisted over the next few months I began to have a clear memory of walking through a field on a very hot day in Texas, when I was about 16 years old. As the sun was beating down on my head, I remembered suddenly knowing, without a shadow of a doubt, that one day I would write a book. It would not be a novel but a "technical" book. While the idea of writing a "technical" book amused me, nonetheless, I just put it in the, "Hmmm, what do you know?" corner of my mind and went on with life.

By mid-2007 the feeling became stronger and stronger. In my meditations I began to "hear" parts of the book and then, one day, I got an intense pain in my right wrist and forearm. The pain felt as if it was actually deep in the bone and was almost constant. Not sure what was going on and having never had this kind of pain before, I went to a friend who is a talented healer and seer and asked her what was going on. She said I had to start writing - immediately. I protested, saying I was not a writer and what would I write about anyway? My friend said I would be given the words.

The book you are about to read are the words I was given over a period of about a year and a half. I realized, early on in the writing, that I was the channel, not the author. Throughout the book you will see references to "we". Now I do not actually know who "we" are, except as I would write I would feel the most wonderful light and powerful energy surrounding me. Often when I was writing (or listening you could say), I would ask who was giving me this information. The same names were repeated each time – Uriel/Uriah and Clarissa. While I still do not know exactly who Clarissa is, I did look up Uriel/Uriah and learned that they are the masculine and feminine aspects of the archangel responsible for, among other things, writing and creativity….seemed appropriate to me! The only thing I can tell you about Clarissa is that she is the most loving, supportive, protective and nurturing energy I have ever felt.

I believe the energies and wisdom of Uriel/Uriah and Clarissa are contained in this book. Almost more important than the words are the energies that come off the page and into the reader's consciousness. So it is a book that is to be both read and felt.

The way the book is organized is exactly the order in which the chapters were given. Each chapter is one day's entry. Only minor changes were made in the process of editing this book. Basically, what you see is the way it was presented to me.

You will undoubtedly notice there are some concepts and sentences that are repeated throughout this book. There is a purpose for this. The first reason is simple – to make sure we "get it" and fully understand a point "they" deem to be of utmost importance. The second is that what follows each repetition gives you a different perspective of a particular point and a higher level of understanding. Each repetition carries with it a deeper energetic flow.

As I wrote this book, the word "god" was mentioned. Sometimes the word "god" would be capitalized and other times not. In the final edit, I decided to go with the conventional and capitalize "God" even though the use of the capitalized word "God" is not referring to god in a religious sense but "God" as a creative force and original essence of all that is.

On a final note, there is no new information in this book, just as there is no new information in the world. The information in this book has been repeated again and again throughout the millennia. This book just presents it in a different way and in a different order that might better appeal to some of you out there.

The ideas contained in this book are not the final truth or the whole truth, just a part of the truth that is relevant today. Take what you like from this book and leave the rest. If there are parts of this book that resonate with you then I am grateful and if there is nothing within these pages that resonates with you, then that is also as it should be.

Everyone's truth is his or her own. No one can tell you what the truth is – only you can know. Finding *your* truth is what the journey of life is all about.

I. Universal Consciousness and the Origins of the Universe

1

Understanding Our Existence

THIS MESSAGE IS UNIVERSAL. It is about the three spiritual keys to understanding the universe and, therefore, our existence: kindness, compassion and love above all other emotions. When we put these emotions first we put ourselves first, and we bring to ourselves the same reaction in others. When we understand our universe, we will understand the purpose of our existence.

Common sense is no longer so common. People spend more time and energy focusing on themselves and their own gain than on the truer principles of life. Energy flows from one being to another – be it from "static" object to "static" object, or from living being to living being. No one and no thing operates in a vacuum. This same concept will be repeated again and again until you hear it and understand its implications.

We are all part of a universal existence. The goal of this existence is to move forward as a whole. We are all parts of the whole but none of us is the whole itself. Therefore, it takes all of us being on the same page, as it were, to move forward. Our individual vision is limited mainly to ourselves, as we are at the center of our own little universes. The key to moving forward is to expand this field of vision and realize we are a part of the whole, and what we think and the actions we take matter, as they affect the whole. The part is definitely not insignificant. Rather the part is significant as it gives shape and substance to the whole.

2

Nothing Is Set in Stone

THERE IS NEVER A BARRIER, invisible or otherwise, between God and humanity. Any such perceived barrier is generated solely on the part of the individual or group working seemingly on behalf of the individual. This barrier is erected out of fear – fear of true humanity or "humanness" and what it really means to be human. Humanness is all about unconditional love, compassion and a true understanding and caring for all that is around you, be it an animal, a rainforest, or a tadpole. This deep-seated compassion frightens many people. This deep-seated compassion threatens many people because it takes away their power to influence, manipulate and control others. Those who express this all-encompassing compassion cannot be controlled or led into wrongdoing by others. The truly compassionate person lives and acts with integrity and gratefulness above all else.

Again, those who wish to control and manipulate others for their own gain or satisfaction operate from a place of destructive ego. Power struggles are inherent in nature but the goal of humans is to rise above this struggle, not succumb to it. We must raise ourselves above the fray of pettiness, jealousy, acts that harm others needlessly, and acknowledge there is a higher source of understanding centered around compassion and a willingness to give to those in need. This giving is not limited to just money, but also time, service, kindness, a thoughtful word or a smile.

Each day we have the opportunity to be a truly compassionate being and rise above the struggle of inhumanity. The future is ours to mold as we will – nothing is set in stone. The universe and everything in it is dynamic, ever-changing energy.

Our thoughts create our reality. Our reality creates our universe. Our universe creates our soul. Does it sound like this order is reversed? It is not. Look at astrology. The position of the planets at our time of birth sets the stage, creates the influences that will shape the timbre of our life events, the timing of such events and our personalities.

It is not we who shape the universe. It is actually a two-way street. Our thoughts create the universe and the universe creates our soul. This is the essence of the universe and the world we live in – there is a constant give and take, or rather a constant give and *receive*. Just as every action against you mirrors some aspect of your thought, so does every thought of yours influence and create some aspect of every action against you.

There is a constant interaction between all thoughts and beings. The universe and everything in it operates as a gentle wave in a small pool – methodically moving back and forth, giving and receiving. Everything is a cycle, a circle without beginning and without end, the alpha and the omega all at once and continually.

When we understand how this flow works we will understand the universe and all her powers of creation, abundance and happiness.

Of course, with this understanding comes a great responsibility to behave correctly and use the power wisely and for the benefit of all and not just oneself. We are again entering into an Age of Enlightenment in which there is the possibility of abundance showering down upon humanity. We are entering into a time of great decisions. Just as there is the constructive ego, there is likewise the destructive ego. It is these egos that will decide the fate of the Earth and world as we currently know it. But fear not, if we don't get it right this time we will eventually have another opportunity – albeit several millennia from now, but an opportunity nonetheless.

Why does this decision come now – why not 1,000 years ago or even 250 years ago? Because we had not yet reached critical mass of thought proliferating the universe. As the number of thoughts increases in the Universal Consciousness we eventually reach critical mass, a point of no return if you will, a time when all the knowledge that ever was and ever will be is in existence and accessible. When we reach this point we as a group must decide how we want to proceed. We have reached this point before yet never decided as a group to proceed along the path of peace and contentment. Instead we have chosen to dissolve ourselves and our earthly reality and start anew. When the time is right to enter into this new phase as a whole we will know it and act upon it. This new phase of existence – and it *is* an existence – will have new parameters and new universal laws for humanity. It will be a higher plane of existence. There will be new challenges and even obstacles in this new phase, just as there are in this phase of existence, but this discussion will be left for another time, perhaps even another book.

What is important at this moment is that you and all who read this book understand you have a choice to make, and your actions and thoughts will speak louder than all the words in Heaven. It is how you behave, think and feel that will determine the outcome – not what you might say or profess to believe. The time for action is now. Do not sit back and do nothing, for if you do the fate you have suffered before will befall you again. You have the power to change your reality and your level of existence. You are free to make whatever choice you feel appropriate. There actually is no right or wrong answer – merely a choice that must be made. This information is being brought to you at this time so you can make an informed decision, so you will be able to be a full partner in creating and co-creating your reality. If you want to start over, we start over. If you want to begin anew at a new level of understanding, we move toward that goal. It is your decision and your creation.

3

We Are All Connected

WHEN YOU FEEL YOU ARE ALONE, you are not. There are hundreds, thousands, millions, of beings from which you can draw energy and sustenance at any moment. These beings have been put on this Earth and in this universe for your benefit and even amusement. Now, when we say "amusement" we do not mean anything cruel or harmful. Rather, we mean "amusement" in such ways that honor this being and treat it with respect and consideration.

You can "contact" or connect with these beings by reaching out with an open and clean heart and touching their energy. It is their energy that will bring you peace, comfort and joy, for these are energetic beings, not physical beings. They are beings of pure light and energy whose sole purpose is to "recharge" your batteries if you will. Recharge in the sense that if you have been feeling down or melancholy there are those among these beings who can make you feel lighter and more optimistic, for that is the specific energy they carry. If you have been feeling fearful or lost, reach out to those beings whose purpose and joy it is to bring you the energy of love and safety.

Make contact with these beings on a daily basis, when you wake up in the morning and before you go to sleep at night. Search your heart as well as your mind for that which you feel needs to be bolstered, and so it shall be done through these beings of light and energy. Just as God has given you the means by which to cure all physical ailments with plants and other natural materials and remedies, so too has God given you the means with which to heal your mental and spiritual ailments through these beings of light energy. These beings can do you no harm. They can, however, protect you from beings from the lesser realms.

The future is yours to create. The future starts now through your thoughts and actions. Think about what you want in your future and begin seeing it, thinking it and acting in such a way so as to bring it about. Actions have consequences. For every action there is an equally powerful reaction. This is a law of nature, a "universal" law in the sense that it applies to every man, woman and child, as well as every creature, plant, molecule and atom in this universe. No one and no thing is immune from the laws of nature. Therefore, know these laws and use them to "our" advantage. This "our" is not a typo, for whatever you think or do affects everyone and everything else via the Universal Consciousness according to the laws of physics. We might think we operate in a vacuum, that no one but ourselves knows our thoughts, but this simply isn't so. We are all connected via the Zero Point Field, Universal Consciousness, Unity Consciousness.

It is the recognition and acceptance of this connectedness that is the purpose of this book. For if we begin to see in real terms how our individual thoughts and actions affect everyone and everything else around us, we might be more willing to initially work on taming and controlling our thoughts, with the eventual aim of being able to direct and focus our thoughts and actions to bring about positive change. We must each take responsibility for the state of our lives and the world as a whole. Again, no one and no thing operates in a vacuum. If you direct loving energy at a plant it will in turn radiate this loving energy back to you – remember, the universe operates on the principle of give and receive. If you give, you will receive – as you sow, so shall you reap. If you receive you will be more willing to give. Study this point and see how it operates in your life. Think hard and observe honestly and you will see the truth of this principle.

No love given is ever wasted. No kind thought or act of compassion is for naught. These thoughts and actions are dispersed into the Universal Consciousness in the form of energy – positive energy – that affects and uplifts all of humanity at a cellular level. This is the principle of universal thought – one thought spurs on another thought and on it goes until that thought finally becomes reality. That thought transforms from the energetic state into the physical or actual state, at least as we currently perceive reality. This is the level of power of a single thought. This is how a single thought is powerful enough to transform war into peace, hatred into love, sadness into joy.

4

Mastering the Cycles

THE END IS NOT NEAR. We are not coming to the end of human existence as we now know it. Rather, we are coming to the end of a cycle of humanity. Humanity flows through stages, which are all part of a larger cycle of life and death. Just as plants, animals and humans have a cycle of life and death, so does humanity. This cycle is known as the wheel of life in some cultures. This wheel is in perpetual motion – it never stops or ceases to exist. Just as this wheel, this cycle, never ceases to exist, neither does humanity. Humanity is always moving and evolving along the cycle of life.

The end is not near. Rather, we are at the beginning of a new cycle of development. One in which we as humans have the power to tap into vast amounts of resources and vast amounts of knowledge from previous times when we have been at this turning point. As mentioned before, this is not the first time humanity as a group has been at the doorstep of such knowledge and spiritual enlightenment. We as a group have made it to this point many times. What we have not done as a group is "crossed over", as it were, into the so-called Promised Land.

We are standing face to face with full understanding of the universe, the power of the Universal Consciousness and spiritual enlightenment. The question is will we get it this time or will we need to go through yet another cycle of destruction, pain and humiliation to get back to this very same point of evolvement and understanding?

So, if we do not want to repeat the cycle what must we do? We must each focus on our own inner development. We must focus on our own spiritual and psychological development and advancement as it issues forth from deep inside us, and not as dictated by those on the outside. We must listen to our hearts and our souls and follow what feels right for each of us. Each person will have a different role to play in moving humanity closer to the gates of Heaven on Earth, which really means a time when there is no suffering on this earthly plane, a time when all people are brothers and sisters and there is no "us" and "them" but just "one".

Because each person will have a different and distinct role to play in moving humanity forward along the path of spiritual enlightenment, it is important that we focus only on ourselves and our own efforts, and not judge what another might be saying or doing. By all means listen and see what they are doing and if it resonates with you, if you feel at your core this is something you believe, add your voice. If, however, after looking deep within your conscience you do not feel this is something you can support, walk away and think of it no more and do not judge it or condemn it. Merely note it and realize it is not for you.

As we move closer to this New Age of spiritual development, there will be an increase in the instances of light meeting dark. There will be more upheaval and tension as well as chaos and destruction. However, this is necessary in order to clear the way for the new level of understanding that will descend upon the Earth. With this new level of understanding will come a new way of thinking and behaving. And this new way of thinking and behaving will create a new universe, a new realm of existence for humanity, a realm of peace, harmony and balance hitherto unknown on this earthly plane. This is the purpose, the very meaning, of existence. This is why we are on this Earth, to bring "home" this new level of understanding and plane of existence.

5

The Future Is Now

THE FUTURE HOLDS GREAT PROMISE for those who wish to see it. For those who wish to experience the coming Golden Age there will be prosperity and abundance hitherto unknown by humankind.

The future is now and is here to do with as you will. The future is not carved in stone but is malleable and can be molded according to your individual thoughts, as well as those of the larger group – all of humanity. We all have a say in how we will proceed because we are all linked via mind and spirit.

The end is not near. We are not at an end but at a beginning – the Age of Enlightenment – an age in which all creatures exist for the betterment and benefit of each other. The individual will cease to be of primary importance. Rather, global issues and the growth and prosperity of the masses will be the main focal point of day-to-day living.

The goal is not material abundance per se but one of spiritual growth and achievement. Our thoughts can aid us in creating this enlightened existence. Remove negative thoughts from your mind by understanding why they are there in the first place, and then extinguishing the source or cause of the dissatisfaction within yourself. Negativity arises from within you. No one causes you to feel sad, angry or happy without your participation and therefore blessing. You alone are responsible for your thoughts and emotional reactions. If someone does something and you feel angry, you must first look within yourself and see what chord of dissatisfaction this person has knowingly or unknowingly tapped. You must then work to understand why you felt angry and go to the root of the anger. Do you feel angry because you feel powerless? Do you feel angry because you feel someone has taken advantage of your goodwill? Or do you feel angry because you feel marginalized and that the other person doesn't care about your feelings?

Once you have identified why this person's actions have caused you to feel angry, you must heal this trigger so this negative emotion will not come up again. Look at your soul and realize you may have been hurt in the past but the present and future are within your control. Take responsibility and heal yourself. Move forward along the path of spiritual enlightenment. Realize you are a child of the Almighty and that all beings are equally perfect and beautiful in the eyes of God. We are all balls of infinitely loving light. What you give out, you shall receive a hundredfold. What is given with a pure heart shall never be rejected. The key is to be able to look within yourself and know whether your actions are pure. Do only that which can be done with a pure heart.

Moving to the next level as a group will require individual effort. The sooner we see we are all linked the better. This linkage is not just between human beings but also between humans and animals, humans and the Earth, and humans and the universe. There is no separation between any forms of existence. All of existence – every being, plant and cell – is linked by energy. This energy is the driving force of the universe and everything in it. We all feed off each other and nurture each other at the same time and continuously.

6

The Aim of Life

THERE IS A MASTER PLAN to the universe. This information is complex and worth delving into if one is to have a better understanding of one's life, its purpose and one's role in humanity and the universe at large. Yes, each and every one of us has not only a life purpose but also a purpose in the universe. Otherwise, our individual thoughts would not have such a direct and deep impact on humanity as well as the universe. The fact that you may not be aware of the role you play is no excuse – it still happens and exists! Ignorance is no excuse. Just as your body functions without your knowing how and without your conscious control does not lessen its existence. The effect you have on the universe is happening whether you know it or not, whether you actively control it or not.

Therefore, imagine how much more of a positive impact you as an individual can have on humanity and the universe if you will just take the time and make the effort to understand how the universe operates and your role in it.

The universe operates in a cyclical fashion. Just as nature is cyclical, so is the universe. What goes up must come down. Where there is good, there is also the potential for bad. Where there is bad, there is ALWAYS the potential for good. Life and the universe are a constant ebb and flow. Sometimes we veer more to the left than the right, and sometimes more to the right than the left. However, what is always true is that in the end we eventually find our way back to a certain balance of nature, a point of equilibrium. Just as the needle of a compass will always point north, so too does humanity and the universe return to a point of equilibrium and harmony.

One of our roles as an individual is to help humanity and the universe return to this point of equilibrium. We do this by having positive thoughts about ourselves and others. This is why it is so important to love others as thyself. When we do this we instill in the universe a positive vibration, a positive frequency that will help the universe, the Earth and everyone on it to return to a level of balanced frequency and energy. This balanced energy is also known as the Christ Consciousness. When this balanced energy returns to Earth in the physical plane we will all once again experience "Heaven on Earth". This is our individual and collective goal.

The aim of life is to return to this natural state of being, this balanced state of being in which all are one and there are no divisions or separateness. The goal is to achieve this on the earthly plane, in physical form.

There are many ways of achieving the necessary knowledge to attain this enlightened state of being, and no way is more beneficial or faster than another. Just as individuals all vibrate at slightly different frequencies, so too do the energies of the methods that have been handed down to achieve enlightenment. As an individual you must choose the path that is best for you, all the while understanding that what is best for you may not be best for another person. We must let go of our negative egos if we are to advance as individuals and as a group. We must set aside our differences and the need to be right. There is no right or wrong when one opens oneself fully to the powers of the universe and its unconditional love and abundance. When your goal is to serve humanity and not yourself you have reached a higher plateau, one in which there is no need for power or self-aggrandizement. You will no longer feel the need to build an altar to yourself to proclaim your individual achievements and sacrifices. Instead, you will glorify humanity and the infinite power of the universe and all within it. You will attain humility and a true understanding of what it means to exist as a human. You will see the true joy of human existence.

Our existence is based on thoughts. These thoughts emit energy and it is this energy that creates and sustains the universe. If our thoughts cease, so does this energy and without this energy there is no universe. Our thoughts are a form of procreation in that they are the building blocks of the universe. The universe and everything within it look as they do because of the thoughts that have accumulated over the ages. Change a thought and you will change the universe. Yes, a single thought is that powerful because like attracts like. One thought will attract another thought of similar energy and these will attract more and more until there is a physical outcome in the form of an explosion or peace. As our thoughts go, so do we. Our thoughts are the building blocks of the universe.

The energy to change the universe lies within each one of us. No one person is more powerful than another. In many of us, this power is dormant.

Some have managed to tap into and activate a small amount of this energy. The key is to purposefully and knowingly tap into this power, activate it and direct it for the greatest benefit of humanity – and by extension the universe – because humanity and the universe are inexorably linked. What we do to the Earth, we do to ourselves. What we do to our neighbor we do to ourselves. The thoughts we have about our neighbors reflect the thoughts we have about ourselves.

7

Moving to a New Level of Perception

We have not reached a plateau as a civilization or a group, rather we have extended the boundaries of our existence. We have extended our thought processes and the relative power and impact of thought to heights unknown by the current inhabitants of Earth. There is no point in recorded time that we as a group have been at such a heightened sense of awareness and stability of mind. It is time to share with other beings this elevated sensory perception that many on Earth currently possess. It is also time to use this elevated sensory perception for the good of all and not just the few.

We can pull ourselves out of the quagmire we are experiencing as individuals, as groups, and even as nations and move beyond it to a new level of perception and perfection. All it will take is a little concentrated effort. We must first move beyond ourselves and see the world in a new light. We must realize the world does not revolve around us as individuals or a group of beings. The universe is there for all to share equally. We must also realize every action we take, every thought we have, affects and influences for better or worse, every other molecule not just on this planet but in the entire universe. When you think about this level of connectedness and really understand it, your perception of yourself as a creator and co-creator takes on a new magnitude, doesn't it? That careless thought about what you wanted to do to the man who cut you off in traffic, or the woman who did not hold the elevator door for you, is not so meaningless now, is it? Random, uncontrolled thoughts of anger, violence, and malice – no matter how insignificant they may seem – have far-reaching implications and influence. You and you alone are responsible for every thought you have, just as you and you alone are responsible for every thought you express and every action you take. There is no one else to blame because you are solely responsible.

Uncontrolled thoughts, just as uncontrolled passion, can kill. Random thoughts of irritation or anger create a frequency equivalent to uncontrolled rage. This uncontrolled rage is then transmitted to every being on the planet via the Universal Consciousness and from there into the universe itself, where – if strong enough – it can even affect the rotation of planets and the formation of stars. Like attracts like and violence begets more violence. The only way to stop the vicious cycle of greed, killing and power struggles is to limit your thoughts to those of love, compassion and mercy.

You can choose your thoughts. You are the gatekeeper of your own mind. Having thoughts of anger and jealousy does not serve you…it does not make you a happier, luckier individual. These thoughts drag you down and attract to you beings and experiences that will bring you sadness and destruction on many levels. There is a dark undercurrent in this universe and this undercurrent feeds off of and is strengthened by every negative thought we have. Negative thoughts and negative emotions will lead to the destruction of humanity. The way to prevent this is to monitor your thoughts and choose carefully which ones you will allow to influence the universe. It all starts with you because you are the gatekeeper of your thoughts. You are also the gatekeeper of your own reality. What beings and experiences will you choose to allow in? It really is up to you.

8

The Greatest Obstacle

Fear of the future and the unknown is the greatest obstacle in the struggle to move forward and progress as a group and a civilization. When fear becomes the predominant emotion guiding our thoughts, impulses and actions it is easy for devastation and destruction to reign, because we begin to focus on our lesser energies and thereby create the least of our potential as humans. By letting these lesser emotions have ascendancy over our higher emotions of love and compassion, we enter into a cycle of destruction and heartache. The lesser emotions are a very powerful force and once unleashed are difficult to control. But these can and must be controlled. They should not be repressed. We must acknowledge their existence and power, but we do not have to feed them and give them even more energy. We need to acknowledge them and then put them aside. We must be vigilant lest they rise up within us again and create once more pain and sorrow on a personal and even national level.

We must focus our thoughts on the positive emotions of love and peace so these thoughts will predominate throughout our lives and throughout the world. The lesser emotions will always exist, but they do not have to be a greater force than that of love and harmony. By bringing a sense of peace and balance to your mind, you will help in bringing these same emotions to everyone else. Positive thoughts create a ripple effect just as negative thoughts do. As the positive thought ripples throughout the Universal Consciousness, it will attract similar thoughts and energies that will eventually materialize and become a concrete reality. But it all starts with a single person – a journey of a thousands miles begins with one step.

9

The Time Is Now

NOW IS THE TIME to look to the future and not to the past. Looking to the past will only serve to rehash old enmities and reopen old wounds. Now is the time to look to the future and realize the promise it holds for those who wish to move forward into a world that is as magnificent as it is wondrous.

The unfolding of the future is at hand for those ready to see beyond the past and the constraints imposed by our own narrow-mindedness and self-centeredness. We stand at the threshold of a new beginning – a threshold beyond which there is peace and tranquility, justice and fairness, balance and humility.

The time for action is now. The time to step up and take hold of the reigns of our own lives and our own realities is now. Gateways and portals into other realms and other modes of existence are opening at a pace unprecedented in our living memory as a group of living, breathing beings. We should rush to take advantage of these openings so we might jump ahead on the wheel of life, the evolution of life, the evolution of human consciousness. The end is not at hand. Rather we stand at a monumental beginning of purpose and existence. Some will agree to go on to this new form of existence and way of being. Others will choose not to proceed at this time. This is fine as it is their choice made of their own free will. Those who do not elect to move forward will revert to an earlier form of creation and begin the cycle of humanity and evolution again. They will go back to square one, so to speak. This is not a step back. It should be viewed as a lateral step – neither good nor bad.

For those who choose to move forward along the wheel of life and existence, a new world and a new universe await. This new world will share many similarities with the one with which we are all familiar. There will, however, be a few notable differences such as the lack of greed, selfishness and *in*humanity. This new world will be a parallel universe in which we will all be free to encourage and develop our higher selves – those higher aspects of our being that have been neglected by so many on this Earth today. This transition will not require physical movement to another planet but rather a shift in our perception of the planet on which we currently live. This other realm is already in existence and is merely shrouded by a paper-thin veil. By venturing to look beyond this veil we will come face to face with this other existence. Many have already dared to go beyond the veil of this existence and many more will follow in the coming few years.

There is nothing to fear about going beyond the veil of our current existence but many fear the unknown. It is this fear of the unknown that will prevent a lot of people from seeing and realizing what is rightfully theirs.

However, once this other side has been viewed, your life will never be the same. It cannot be.

10

Achieving Your Life's Purpose

THE SOUL KNOWS where it belongs and where it is to go. An issue often comes up when we attempt to consciously direct our soul. By consciously directing our soul according to materialistic needs and desires, we often veer off our life path and our life becomes full of discord and suffering. What we thought we wanted no longer seems to have the same appeal once we get it, be it a car, a spouse, money or even a child! We cannot look to things or other people to bring about our soul's purpose. People and events along the way can help you see more clearly perhaps by illuminating certain aspects you need to look at more closely or rethink, but they by themselves cannot bring you happiness. Happiness is achieving your life's purpose – attaining the goals your higher self has set out for you in this lifetime.

Many people have a deep-seated sense of failure even though by societal standards they are successful. This is because they have not achieved their life's purpose. One can be successful in terms of job and money but if the soul has not been nourished, if the soul's true life path has not been at least acknowledged, much less attained, the victory will be a hollow one and the person will always have a longing deep in their heart for something they cannot identify.

Of course, achieving one's life purpose and being successful according to the dictates of society are not mutually exclusive. They only become so when one is achieved at the expense of the other. To achieve both there needs to be a balance, an equilibrium of focus. Before taking any action you must know what your soul has to say about it. Listen to your soul and your heart because they will never lead you astray. Your mind, on the other hand, will. Your mind is susceptible to outside influences, to negative emotions and to pettiness, whereas your soul is above this. Your soul communes directly with God and has nothing to prove and nothing for which it must get revenge. The goal of every soul is to achieve balance and harmony on this physical plane we call Earth. We are all trying to achieve balance and harmony in our thoughts, in our actions and in our minds. One of the most efficient ways to achieve this goal is by service to humanity.

By giving to others we give to ourselves. We all have the same purpose; we just carry it out in different ways. Whether we help others by raking leaves, or leading a country, or being a sales clerk, we all have the same potential to affect humanity in a positive way. We all come into contact with people on a daily basis and it is what you make of this contact that affects humanity. No encounter is meaningless. Every encounter generates a thought and an emotion that filters out into the Universal Consciousness. Now, will this thought, this emotion, be a positive one that moves humanity closer to fulfilling its group aim of peace and prosperity, or will it be a negative thought and a negative emotion that will pull humanity – and you, of course – further away from balance and harmony?

Some of you will say that the fate of the world could hardly hang on a single negative thought, but it does. This is the magnitude of power behind a single careless thought. Thoughts are energy and according to universal laws like attracts like. Your one negative thought may be the thought that breaks the proverbial camel's back and plunges us into darkness and chaos. On the other hand, your single positive thought may be the one that opens up a new realm of existence for humanity – a realm characterized by love, peace, abundance and harmony.

Humanity is at a crossroads. Our fate is in our hands. There will be no demons from the netherworld that will rise up and lead us to destruction. Neither will there be benevolent aliens from outer space who will miraculously come to our rescue. No, we are responsible for what happens next. We, as a group, will determine whether we proceed along the path leading to enlightenment, or we call it quits and start over, hoping to get it right next time.

We must take full responsibility for the outcome of our existence. If we want to move along the path of enlightenment, we must learn to control our thoughts. Thoughts create the physical world. So, instead of running around trying desperately to put out fires that spring up, let's work on preventing the fires in the first place by controlling and directing our thoughts toward love, balance and harmony. By removing judgment of ourselves and others from our thoughts we remove pain and suffering.

11

A Higher Level of Existence

GRATITUDE MAKES THE WORLD GO ROUND and is the cornerstone of a happy life. Expressed gratitude helps thoughts become physical more quickly. The quicker a positive thought can materialize into the physical world, the quicker we can change the world in which we live. Gratitude is the nucleus around which the universe orbits. The more the gratitude, the faster the universe spins. The faster the universe spins, the more good that can be done on this earthly plane and the higher the level of existence we can reach as a group and a species.

Nothing is for naught. No thought or action is ever wasted. Everything in this universe serves a higher purpose. That purpose is the evolution of humanity. We are trying as a group to get to the next higher level of existence – we just don't realize it. The next higher level of existence is one in which there are no wars, pain or suffering. It is a universe in which peace, balance, harmony and happiness reign supreme. It is a place in which people will look inwardly and not outwardly to find deep satisfaction and peace of being. It is a place in which people will focus more on nurturing their souls than their bank accounts (there will be no bank accounts!). It is a place in which the true dictates and principles of humanity will be exhibited and followed by the occupants.

The time for the transition to this new level of existence is now. We are standing at a crossroads. Which direction the future will take is fully in our hands. Which direction we take at this crossroads is our choice.

There is, however, a higher power upon which we can call to receive guidance and help in meeting this challenge and crossing over into this new level of existence.

12

The Keys Are within Your Grasp

THE EVOLUTION OF HUMAN CONSCIOUSNESS requires each of us to take a stand and know what we believe. We must also understand what we believe, because belief without true understanding is an empty shell. We have to know and understand how the universe operates and why the universal laws function as they do. By having a true understanding of how the world in which we live operates, we can change our lives and the world. We can use the laws of nature and the laws of the universe to create the world in which we want to live. We can use these laws to help others gain a better understanding of themselves and the world in which they live. At this point in time, there is no great mystery that is beyond our understanding. All "laws" are clearly written and the information needed to understand them is within our grasp – all we have to do is reach out and embrace it.

Those of pure mind, body and spirit will be the first to be able to reach out and grasp this understanding, which we can call the keys of the universe. "Pure" does not mean perfect. None of us are perfect, but those who have a pure intention toward humanity are as close to perfection as we can currently get at this level of conscious development. In the next level of existence we will of course be able to get much closer to perfection, but we will discuss this further in a later chapter.

There is no need to strain to understand the keys of the universe. The comprehension of the keys will be as easy as adding 2+2 once one has reached a certain level of spiritual development. The strain, the effort, will take place as one strives to reach the necessary point of spiritual development. If someone else presents the keys of the universe to you and you do not understand them, you need to focus on your own spiritual development and evolution and not jump ahead to the keys. This is somewhat of a safety device because an insufficiently evolved person could do great harm with the keys.

The keys are powerful and a misapplication of them could destroy the universe in seconds.

The keys contain limitless energy. Understanding how this energy flows gives the power to alter this flow by either intensifying or decreasing it. This is how physical matter is manipulated.

13

Think of Others as You Would
Have Them Think of You

THE TIME HAS COME that we should not only *do* unto others as we would have them *do* unto us, but we should take it one step further and also *think* of others as we would have them *think* of us.

Thoughts have power. They have the power to create and to kill. The sooner we accept this the better because when we accept this reality, we will be able to use our thoughts to create harmony, peace and balance in our lives and in the universe.

Energetic beings create by using their own energy, by directing their energy into specific patterns. Knowledge of specific patterns and ways of formulating energy are now being downloaded into people and the Earth itself. This knowledge has not been seen on Earth in millions of years, but the time has come for this information to resurface. With this knowledge, humans will be able to create a completely new existence, one of balance, peace and harmony.

Of course, this information can also be used to destroy the Earth if it is misused by greedy, corrupt individuals. The information is available to all. Information and knowledge are neutral – it is what we choose to do with information that makes it either "good" or "bad". Results are what we need to scrutinize and focus upon, not the information itself. Know what it is you desire, focus on the outcome you want and the rest will be taken care of. Focusing on what it is you want to create will direct energy into that pattern. Once energy is directed into that pattern it will become a physical reality. As soon as you focus on the desired outcome the process of manifestation begins and it is already complete. However, few people on Earth today are able to see beyond the physical, three-dimensional realm, so they do not believe the desired outcome has been achieved until they see the actual physical manifestation. Knowing something is complete before you see it manifested in the physical speeds the process along.

The more strongly we are connected to the Universal Consciousness, i.e., all the thoughts and knowledge that has ever existed, the faster we will be able to make our thoughts into physical reality. Just as food nourishes the body, meditation nourishes the soul. Meditation helps us connect with the universe and the universal laws. The universal laws are the body of knowledge through which we create our physical reality.

The universal laws are open to everyone but few people pay attention to them and practice them. Read about the universal laws, understand the universal laws and do your best to implement them. However, remember the prime directive: *Do* unto others as you would have them *do* unto you; *think* of others as you would have them *think* of you. By keeping this directive at the forefront of your mind, you will be able to avoid misusing the powerful information that is now readily available to all of humanity. It is adherence to this directive that will prevent humanity from destroying itself again.

If you remember nothing else in this book, remember this: **Do** unto others as you would have them **do** unto you; **think** of others as you would have them **think** of you.

14

Energy Is Thought in Motion

THE TIME HAS COME for the secrets of the universe to be shared with humankind. The secrets will be revealed in a step-by-step manner that will enable the "user" to harness the energy of the universe and direct it for the benefit of humankind. The time of wars and strife involving individuals and nations is at an end. Henceforth, Earth will be a place of serenity and harmony, of love and compassion.

Peace is at hand if we will but reach out and grab hold of it, as we have grabbed hold of death and destruction in the past. Focus on the power of thought, meditate on the power of thought and help bring this new level of existence into the physical plane. Focusing on positive energies does not mean burying one's head in the sand and refusing to acknowledge the negative forces in this world. Rather, focus on the positive while acknowledging the negative. Use the power of the positive to overcome the power of the negative. Refusing to see the negative gives more power to negative forces, while using the power of the positive in a purposeful and direct manner can actually neutralize the negative.

Energy is thought in action. Energy is thought in motion. Energy is in constant motion, which means we have the opportunity to change our reality at any moment and at every moment. The significance of this statement is that we hold reality in the palms of our hands and yet we don't even realize it. Energy is constantly swirling around us. We feel life pushes us forward and into new circumstances, yet we are the ones propelling ourselves forward with our thoughts, which create energy, which create our physical reality. If we direct our thoughts, we will direct the energy swirling around us and thereby direct the world that is created. The interchange between thoughts, energy and physical creation is constant. There is not one moment in time in which we do not create our own reality with the power of our thoughts.

15

Emotions Create Your Reality

MEDITATION NURTURES THE SOUL by briefly taking us out of our highly compacted bodies. For the brief time we are meditating, we are able to once again connect with the realms from which we originated. We are able to feel the lightness and the joy of being. We are able to be carefree once again and to see the higher purpose of life on this planet.

Emotions are real. Emotions tell us what is going on in our heads and in our bodies. Emotions are not make-believe nor are they just byproducts of a larger cause. Emotions are real and very physical energies. Emotions create physical reality whether we are aware of it or not. This is one of the universal laws. Your emotions create your reality. By learning to control your emotions you will be in the driver's seat when it comes to controlling your reality and the people, places and events that form your reality.

Focusing on happy, positive emotions will bring more joy and contentment into your life. It will also bring more FUN into your life. Focusing on negative emotions will bring more suffering and trauma into your life. "Focusing" means hanging onto and feeding these emotions by letting them continue and occupy a larger portion of your thoughts and thought patterns. You have a choice – we ALL have a choice – about what thoughts occupy our minds. Therefore, we all have a choice as to which emotions occupy our bodies and thereby create our reality. There are truly no victims in this world. Your higher self may choose to experience certain "unpleasant" realities while on this planet; however, what you make of that experience and how you use that experience to further you along the path of enlightenment is, of course, up to you. This is a very difficult concept for humans to understand and integrate, but the time will come when there will no longer be any need to experience "unpleasant" events.

We are moving toward a time of "Heaven on Earth". This of course is not an end. Humanity will continue to evolve. Human consciousness will continue to grow and expand in ways the present human mind cannot at this point comprehend. The universe is truly limitless and so is the capacity of the human consciousness to evolve.

As humans, we like to set boundaries and limits. We tend to feel more comfortable operating in confined spaces. However, it is now time to listen to the Universal Consciousness and break free of self-imposed restrictions on our thoughts. It is time to open our minds to the Universal Consciousness and explore the new world that is out there. There are no limits. The only limits are those that we impose on ourselves or allow others to impose on us. We create our own reality. We are in charge of our thoughts and emotions. It all depends on how we choose to look at "it", at life. The glass can be half full or half empty. You can take steps to nurture good health and positive thought patterns, or you can do your body and mind harm by holding onto negative patterns.

You can build a wall around yourself and prevent yourself from being in touch with the Universal Consciousness and all the gifts it has to give you, or you can take the necessary steps to unlock your mind and free yourself from worry and negative patterns. You can open your heart and mind and have constant access to the wonder known as the Universal Consciousness. There is no need for suffering and hatred.

The end is not near. We are at the start of a new beginning.

16

Truth or Destruction – You Decide

THE DAY IS NOT DONE. Time is not finished. There are avenues of release and relief which have not yet been explored. This is what we are here to do at this point. We are here to look at ways of evolving and solving problems that we have not yet considered. There are still many options available to humanity. There are still many ways to pull ourselves off the road of doom and destruction. The end is not near. We have said this many times and we are saying it again. There is no need to panic. However, humanity must stop and take a serious look at what is going on. Humanity must now decide which direction it wants to move in. That is the issue really. In which direction do you want to go? We can go "backward" to a time that is less complex and hectic. We can go "forward" to a time that is more universal where truths not only exist but are followed. Or we can go to a place of destruction and darkness. These are just a few of the choices available to humanity, and now is the time the decision must be made.

17

Think Yourself into Magnificence

GRATITUDE IS THE CORNERSTONE of an abundantly happy and successful life. Give thanks for what you have and what you do not have, and by so doing you will be able to control what flows into your life and what flows out of your life.

Thought is life and life is thought. Just as actions speak louder than words, thought speaks the loudest of all, because thought is where the entire process begins. All actions, all words, all emotions, begin with a single thought. Therefore, learning to control our thoughts will enable us to control the outcome, to direct and influence not only our own lives but the world around us.

The world we live in is a magnificent place full of abundance and wonder. It is up to us as individuals to tap into this flow of consciousness and elevate the development of humanity and bring a higher vibration to this planet, which will benefit all who are in existence.

18

It Is All Here Now

THE UNIVERSE IS HERE NOW. All that we see and all that we experience are bits and pieces of the universe. Reality is here and now. There is no separation between man and reality, between man and the universe, between man and the Universal Consciousness. All that is and all that will be are at our disposal 24 hours a day. All that ever was and all that shall ever be is here with us now. There is no separation between past, present or future. All is now. The separations are only in our minds.

19

Trust Yourself

THE END IS NOT NEAR and all is not lost on this planet. The end will come in its own time but not now or anywhere near now. The end is not near but the beginning is. The beginning is the start of something wondrous and beautiful – a world so peaceful and harmonious we cannot at this moment in time actually conceive of such peace and tranquility. The start of a new resonance and world order is in the process of beginning now. All we have to do to experience this glorious existence is to reach out and touch it. It is that easy. The transition to this new energy and way of being is that easy to attain. You do not have to spend years meditating or sitting in a cave. All you have to do is reach out and touch it because this energy is all around you now. It is there for the taking if you are willing to break with the past, to let go of old mindsets and old ways of thinking and behaving.

The end is not near but the beginning is. Reach out and take hold of the new way of existing and you will never look back with remorse or regret, for all you have ever needed or ever will need will be at your feet. The flow of abundance will be continuous and without hesitation. All will be yours in a heartbeat if you will only trust yourself and come over to the other way of being and existing.

20

Every Decision Is Perfect

JUST AS THERE ARE NO MISTAKES in the universe so there are no wrong decisions in life. Every decision we make is perfect for that moment and every moment after that point. There is something called the knock-on effect, which means there are consequences to every action and reaction, every decision and every thought. Sometimes we think we have made a wrong choice and are filled with regret, but this is not the correct use of our minds. The choice we make today may lead to what seems to be an undesirable outcome, but this simply is not the case because there are no wrong choices. It is impossible in the grand scheme of things to make a bad choice or a wrong decision.

Every decision we make leads to a chain reaction of events. A single decision you make today may lead to world peace or a cure for cancer. Of course you may never be able to trace your one decision to this final outcome, but all thoughts and ideas on this planet are tied to each other. No one thought or idea exists in isolation; every action and reaction can be traced back to another thought or reaction. Thoughts build upon each other until finally there is some sort of physical outcome, a physical reality if you will. And this physical reality helps to create the groundwork for more thoughts, more decisions, more choices and more actions and reactions in this world. Thoughts and decisions build layer upon layer until finally there is a physical reality connected to them, an "outcome", a "result" that is tangible and understood by everyone. However, what is not always understood or even considered are the thoughts and decisions that led up to that outcome.

By ignoring the thoughts and decisions that have led to certain outcomes we are denying responsibility for our thoughts and actions. We are operating in perpetual reaction to events and circumstances, rather than being proactive in creating our own circumstances and the world in which we want to live. And yes, one person and just one single thought can make all the difference in the world...and can save the world and this planet.

We have said this before and we will say it again, a single thought is all that stands between complete destruction and complete harmony. A single thought has such power because one thought begets another thought and another and another, until finally there is a consequence, a physical manifestation of that thought that impacts your world and mine. Just as no man is an island, no thought ever occurs in isolation.

Monitor your thoughts and direct them in a positive manner if you want to improve your life and that of those around you. We are not asking you to direct your thoughts to making more money or getting that promotion at work. We are asking you to remove negative thinking and negative patterns from your thoughts in order to create a more harmonious, more balanced and more enlightened society and planet. This is not about your micro needs but about the continued existence and evolution of the planet as a whole. How much money you make today or whether you get that new car is irrelevant to the evolution of humanity. Abundance is there for all who wish to receive it; not all wish to receive it for various reasons. Don't waste your time and energy focusing on abundance. Rather, focus your time and energy on making a difference in this world and this universe, by helping this planet to ascend to the next higher lever of existence. Focus your efforts on helping humanity pull itself up to the next higher level of existence. Then you will have achieved something. Then you can look back and say you made a positive contribution and had a positive impact on this world.

In the end you will not be judged according to the negative impact you might have had on the world, but on the positive contribution you made to humanity while in physical form. You will be judged according to what you did right and not what you did "wrong" because there are no wrong decisions, there are no bad choices. But there are decisions and choices that are clearly in the higher interests for yourself and humanity, and these are the criteria upon which you will be judged. Actually, when your physical life is over you will judge yourself according to what you set out to accomplish in the life you just lived.

21

Seeing Reality as It Is

THIS IS THE DAY to begin a new thought process, a new way of looking at and perceiving life and the events that go on around us. From today forward you will no longer look at the world in the same way. You will see reality for all its faults and all its glories as it was meant to be seen and perceived by humanity. For many of you this will come as a surprise, and for many of you it will be the next logical step on the road to self-evolution and self-fulfillment. Many of you have been waiting for this day with eager anticipation. Regardless of whether this day comes as a shock or as a long-awaited event, all will benefit from the changing times.

The perception with which we view the world will change – it must change. We have to start looking at the world with new eyes, with fresh eyes that can see accurately and plainly the pain and suffering that is going on in the name of God, religion and nationhood. We must now begin to see that what we are doing and what we have been doing is a lie. We are doing nothing for God because God needs nothing from us. We are doing nothing for religion because religion is not real, but merely a powerbase for control and oppression. We are doing nothing for our nations because our nations are made up of people and I ask you – what is your nation doing for humanity? How is your nation contributing to the evolvement of the human race? Is your nation contributing to the evolvement or devolvement of the human race? If your answer is the latter, you must now do something to change the tide. It is up to you, one person, and that person's thoughts…even just one thought can make a difference to humanity. A single thought can ensure humanity's survival and evolvement.

II. The Way Forward – Choosing Our Future

22

A Shared Responsibility

THE WAY FORWARD for humanity is already quite clear and apparent. We must change the way we view humanity. Instead of viewing humanity as a teeming mass of people with a "kill or be killed" attitude, we need to look at our fellow humans as beings of light and love. We need to view ourselves and our neighbors as creatures who have needs and desires, but the overriding thought before any action is taken should be, *Will this action, will my action, harm another person in any way?* If the answer is *Yes*, you must not take that action. You must find another way to settle the dispute, or you must abandon the thought/action completely. Harm comes in many forms – from the physical to the psychological to the emotional – and if your action and its underlying thought will cause harm to another being you must stop that action and its underlying thought. This is how the world will be saved from itself. This is how we will continue to exist and to evolve as a group.

Again, we are all responsible for our thoughts as well as our actions. There are no victims in this world, other than those who fail to recognize that we are all responsible for our thoughts and actions. While we all have responsibility for our individual thoughts and actions, we also share responsibility for the thoughts and actions of those around us, whether or not we know them personally. My thoughts influence your thoughts, just as your thoughts influence my thoughts. And just as my actions influence your actions, your actions influence my actions. However, the time has come for each of us to own up to our individual and group responsibilities. If someone is rude to you, if someone makes a snide comment about you, ignore it and send this person love from the bottom of your heart. Send this love willingly and gratefully knowing your action, this single action, has the potential to prevent an escalating cycle of negativity, which ultimately leads to violence and murder in one form or another.

This is not the end of the story. We can take this a step further and describe how a single molecule, a single atom, can change the world. Nuclear fusion occurs when a single atom strikes and collides with another atom. This instigates a chain reaction which ultimately ends in a massive explosion of energy that not only destroys people and buildings, but also devastates the environment. This extreme and sudden explosion of energy also releases large amounts of anger and hatred into the atmosphere and into the Universal Consciousness. After all, what thoughts are behind the setting off of a nuclear device? It could be nothing short of hatred and vengeance. No country would detonate a nuclear device in order to *help* humanity. No, the only reason one would commit such a crime would be to destroy another. There can be no "right" or "honorable" intentions behind the detonation of a nuclear device, or any type of bomb or tool of death and destruction.

We are still grappling with the anger and fear and need to dominate released by the atomic devices set off over Japan in World War II.

The time has come to begin to reverse this trend and to neutralize these negative thoughts and energies, so we can move forward on the evolutionary scale. The time has come to put these atrocities behind us and to do what we can to create a more positive, optimistic and better way of living and being.

23

Changing Our View of Humanity

THE WORD "HUMANITY" has many meanings and connotations. To some, "humanity" is a mass of people who have little or no direction in their lives and little or no connectedness to one another. Each man, woman and child is indeed an island lost in the sea of humanity. Each person is tossed to and fro by the waves and gales of life. In this view, there is little hope, faith or love. In this view there is evil, darkness and despair.

To others, "humanity" represents a group of sentient beings who actively participate in creating and running their lives and the direction their futures, both individually and collectively, will take. This is the version of humanity we will focus on at this moment. This is the type of humanity who can help take us forward into the dark days ahead with joy in our hearts and faith in our connectedness and ultimate lightness and Godliness. We are all closer to God than you realize. We, each of us, stand at the right hand of God. We each do His bidding and absorb His wisdom and goodness with each breath we take. This is not to say we are separate from God. Rather, we are all a part of God in God's infiniteness. We are all truly God in our own right. Sometimes we take turns standing at God's right hand and other times we take turns being God itself, being the ultimate creator of all things good and just. There is no separation between God and humanity. Humanity as a whole is good and just, fair and balanced.

However, sometimes we lose sight of our goodness and our justness and step into territory that brings only pain and shame, upon ourselves and humanity at large. We are currently standing in such territory. We have lost sight of what it means to be human. We have lost sight of what it means to help others with an open heart, looking for no reward and seeking no justification for our actions. We have stepped into a land where the name of the game is money and to succeed at all costs, and if I succeeded you could have succeeded and the fact that you didn't shouldn't keep me awake at night, because I paid my dues and now I am reaping what is rightfully mine. But is it? How did you come by that job that put you at the top of the corporate ladder? How did you come by that education that opened the doors of Wall Street to you? How did you come by that chance meeting in the 5th grade with that person at the ice cream parlor who filled your head with the dream to be a superstar? The person who told you, you could be anything you wanted to be, all you had to do was wish hard enough and believe strong enough and it would all be yours? Do you really think all of these random events were by chance? Do you really believe all of the breaks you had in life were created only by you with the intention of benefiting only you?

With greater awareness comes greater responsibility because the more we know, the more we realize the impact each and every one of us, the impact each and every thought, can have on our lives and on humanity itself. In the same vein, with greater riches and power comes greater responsibility. With more money and more power, you have a greater responsibility to help those in need. Do you think for a minute that if our great political leaders and great corporate leaders had been thinking along these lines we would be living in a world always seemingly on the brink of war in one region or another? Do you think we would be living in a world in which most of us in the name of "security from terrorists" live in a police state where we have no real right to privacy and freedom of information? Do you think it is necessary to control information and movement of people in a world that abides by the principle of responsibility toward our neighbors as well as to self?

This is the world in which we live – we lock our doors, secret away our valuables, live under threat that some suicide bomber will set off a bomb at our partner's workplace or near our children's school. We live in a world where more than half the population does not know where its next meal is coming from. And yet at the same time we have pockets of wealthy, powerful individuals and cartels (corporate as well as political) in EVERY country on this planet that do nothing to help the less fortunate. We look down on those who are less fortunate and who are poor or unemployed as if they have done something wrong to have become part of the teeming masses of poor. It must be something they did, be it in another life or in this one, or so we tell ourselves. They are only getting what they deserve, as many of the richest and most powerful amongst us would have us believe. But what if these teeming masses of poor were actually the ones closest to God and all that God stands for? What if the richest and most powerful among us, by their actions (or lack of action to help end the suffering of the poor and decrepit) are closest to the concept of pure evil we know on this planet today? How can we say a powerful nation who chooses to spend its national wealth on weapons of destruction and a military force to invade other countries, when their rulers no longer serve our needs, is just and fair?

How can we say an individual leader who knowingly and willingly deprives others of proper medical care, or a proper education, or the opportunity to put food on the table, because this leader thinks the money and resources are better spent on weapons and the means of war is just and fair? There is very little on this planet at this point that is just and fair. It is not that 50, 100, 200 years ago things were more just or fair. Throughout history we have had the problem of people thinking they were God, behaving as if they have the right to decide who will live and die and in what manner they will live and die, without understanding the principle of God or the responsibility that comes with the power of creation, the power to create reality, the true power of being God.

We have become a world that has cut itself off from the source of life, as well as the meaning of life. Life was never meant to be a struggle, never meant to be an "us or them" paradigm in which your gain is my loss. Life was never meant to be a competition. Life was meant to be a harmonious balancing of energies and ideas, of strange and wondrous moments where we caught glimpses of our power to create and the light of God within each of our souls. We were supposed to use our minds to fend off negative emotions and thoughts. We were supposed to harness the power of love in this universe and use it to create a Heaven on Earth within this dense dimension. We have been striving to create a world where there is no suffering, where there is no greed. We have been trying to create a world where life is dominated by love and compassion, truth and beauty, where there is no deception on any level.

This was the goal when we set out on this adventure hundreds of millions of years ago. How do you think we did? Are we closer to this objective today than we were 10 years ago, 20, 150, 300? What is your heart's desire today? What was your heart's desire when you were four years old, when you were 16? How is today's heart's desire different from that when you were four? Which desire is more pure? Which is more likely to bring you a better understanding of the universe and your place in it? Which desire bears more markings of the society in which you live and values that society places on things? Which desire is truly more from your heart and which is more from what society tells you is good for you and will bring you happiness? Look around you, how many truly happy people do you know? How many people do you know who consistently wake up with a song of joy in their heart and the joy of being alive? How many people do you know who love humanity, each and every one of them?

We are shaped by the society in which we live. Perhaps it is time to step back and ask if what society is teaching us is leading to greater happiness on an individual and collective level. If the answer is *No* perhaps it is time to step out of the constraints of society and live life according to your own beliefs and thoughts. Perhaps it is time for each of us to live life according to the way we think will bring the maximum joy to ourselves *and others* around us. If something brings you lasting joy (not the fleeting kind of "joy" that comes from buying a new car or eating a fine dinner with expensive wine) – the kind of joy that makes your heart sing 12 years after the fact, it is guaranteed to bring joy to others.

24

A New Dawn

WHY ARE WE HERE, on this planet and at this time? Why would any of us choose to be here, on this planet and at this time when the "dark days" of the soul are looking us directly in the eye? Why would we want to go through such suffering or witness such suffering? For the same reason Jesus Christ allowed his physical body to be persecuted and killed, because we, humanity, are on the verge of a transformation as a group. Jesus and Buddha brought new energies to Planet Earth. They brought with them the energies of unconditional love and compassion. They brought with them the energies of forgiveness and tolerance. Because of the density of the prevalent energies at the time of Jesus and Buddha, the world could absorb only a small amount of these newer, lighter energies and not be thrown off balance.

However, in the years that have passed since the time of Jesus and Buddha believe it or not we as a group have made great progress in lightening the energetic sequence of the planet, and are therefore ready to plunge headlong into a transformative stage in which the old ways of thinking, feeling, behaving and loving will fade away. The old ways will be replaced with an entirely new and light form of energy. Of course, the process of transformation will not necessarily be easy for most of us. It will be like trying to break an old habit and replace it with a healthier one. The deal is, we have been addicted to these particular habits for centuries...so it is going to take some awfully cold turkey to kick these habits! But doable it is and as you will see, well worth the effort. By the time you get to the other side, which will be just a few short years, you will look back at your old way of thinking and behaving and just shake your head in wonder at how you could have been so blind and uncomprehending. A new dawn awaits humanity.

25

We Are Part of the
Greater Plan

FOREVER IS BUT A DROP in the bucket of time. Forever stretches from here to eternity and back…many, many times. Time is an artificial construct developed by humans to help place themselves within the structure they know as the universe. The universe and all that is within it is timeless and spaceless. Space too is an artificial construct developed by humans to place themselves within the structure they know as the universe. Reality as humans know it does not exist. Instead there is an ageless, timeless, spaceless universe "out there" in which humans are but one small, tiny, infinitesimal piece. The universe expands beyond humankind's ability to comprehend. Just because you cannot comprehend something does not mean it does not exist. Likewise just because you cannot comprehend something does not mean you should have blind faith and trust that it does exist. Often people are led astray by those who say this is too big and complex for you to understand, so just have faith that what I am telling you is true and all will be okay. No, this is not the truth. It will not be okay. If you do not understand something how can you have belief or faith in it? How can you know its origins and the truth of its being/existence if you do not make an effort to understand the concept behind the truth?

That is what meditation does. It helps us ascertain the truth behind the myth. It helps us to see the truth of our origins and our beginnings. It helps us to piece together why we are here and the role and purpose we serve in this world, and how we can further help humanity move along its path to a greater understanding of itself and the universe.

Why is it important that humans understand the universe and the origins of themselves and the universe? The truth of these concepts will not be hidden forever. It will soon be time for these truths to be known to a wider circle of beings and when this time occurs, which is in the very near future, the world will be forever changed as will everything within this known universe. There is a greater plan to this universe than man knows or can comprehend today. However, it will not always be hidden from him/her, for she/he has a great and wondrous role to play in enacting the catalyst that will set the ball in motion. The truth behind this catalyst will soon appear and when it does a light more brilliant than ever imagined will shine down on Earth and bask its inhabitants in love, peace and harmony. When this truth shall appear there will be rejoicing and singing in the streets unlike anything you have ever seen in your many lifetimes. You will feel the full and complete blessing of the one whom you call God. You shall experience unheard-of riches and glory as a race – the human race. You shall dwell in this state for many millennia as was part of the pact you made when you all started on this journey millennia ago. The journey has been long and hard for some of you but the times of trouble and tribulation will soon end, and when they do you will know true joy for the first time in many millions of years. You all have done your jobs exceptionally well and we are proud of each and every one of you. By your efforts we will all ascend to a new level of being and happiness, for as above so below and *as below so above*. You see, the world is much more complex than you can comprehend.

26

The Way Forward as a Group

THE WAY TO THE FUTURE is clear for those of you who care to see it. We have hidden nothing from you, nor have we made it so difficult that only a select few of you will be able to pass through to the next side. The way forward is clear and it is understandable by a great number of you.

The future stretches before you in a long maze of events and chain reactions. These chain reactions have already been set in motion and will become clearer as time moves forward. These chain reactions are nothing to fear but rather should be embraced, since they are what will catapult humanity into the ranks of the angels and beyond. Yes, humanity will be elevated to the ranks of angels while still here on Earth. This is what establishes the understanding of Heaven on Earth that many of you have been so eagerly awaiting. How else did you think this energy would be anchored on this planet if not by the angelic beings many of you will become?

What will come to pass and how it will come to pass is the next question you will ask, correct? Yes. There will be a series of mishaps in the world economy that will force people to go back to their roots in the sense that they will have to depend on others as well as God for their survival. Through this they will realize that indeed no man is an island nor can one man (or man alone) exist without a connection to others. And "others" in this case means other beings of light as well as humanity and the Earth itself.

Without the appropriate connection to Mother Earth, humans will not survive. For too long now man has removed itself from this circle of connection and light and has convinced itself that he alone is master of the universe and of all he surveys. This concept and perception of the world is completely false. It is also very negative in that it brings in negative energies because it separates man from God, the universe and the true energy of life. Humanity has been withering on the vine for decades now. Yes, a certain amount of decay and withering has been in progress for centuries but in the last seven decades man has managed to crank up the rate of decay to a phenomenal degree – a degree that was indeed our "worst case scenario" for humanity. For this we congratulate you all, but now the party is over and it is time to pay the piper for your past actions and mindless destruction of Planet Earth and all that sits and depends upon this planet. You see humanity is not the only group of beings that depend upon Earth for its survival. There are many other races and groups of beings that have a stake in what happens on Planet Earth. Their very survival in some cases is linked to the survival of not only this planet but also the human race. Your extinction means their extinction.

It was set up this way so man on Earth could redeem itself for grave and serious mistakes made in past eons – eons that are no longer a part of your known history, yet are still a part of your DNA and collective unconscious. It is this collective unconscious that now drives some of you to seek solace in prayer and meditation, and it is a strong connection to this collective unconscious that will propel some of you forward and help you to lead those who are close to "getting it" but are not quite there yet. Nobody who truly believes in what is to come will be left behind.

What were these past mistakes? The wanton killing and mutilation of people and animals for sport and show. Runaway egos that made some people think they were greater than the source of all creation and existence. There is such an energy although very few people are ever fully aware of it or are able to tap into its full magnificence and glory. Unbridled greed was another grave mistake made by humans in past eons. Many of the traits and characteristics you see popping up around you over the last 70 or so years are similar to the "mistakes" made in the past. Now, crank up the intensity of the current negative emotions and actions by a factor of 1,000, and you will get an idea of how far humanity descended into the depths of its own hell in the past.

This will not be allowed to repeat itself. The experiment will be cut short rather than have this sort of behavior once again pollute the universe. However, because man has been through this part of the experiment before, you actually have a bit of a heads up in terms of what to expect and how to sidestep the really negative, ugly parts. That's why we say it is make-or-break time for humanity. You have repeated this experiment so many times, but have been unable to make the leap into the angelic realms while still on this planet, in this density and dealing with so much negativity.

Man has either been unable or unwilling to let go of what is familiar, even though what is familiar is dragging you down the pit of hell of your own making. It has been decided on high that if humanity cannot make the leap this time, it will never be able to make the jump. We mention this not as a threat but as a warning that you as a group must try your best this time. We also mention this because we have seen you reach this point many times and we truly feel you will make it into the next realm this time. We have full and complete confidence in your ability to transcend the darkness of your own soul and come fully into the light of knowledge, compassion and unconditional love.

27

Surviving the Times to Come

SIGNS OF THE TIMES TO COME – which are actually here upon you (humanity) now. There will be signs by which you can gauge the progress of humanity in its goal to reach a higher evolutionary stage. These signs are temporal markers for your eyes only, as it were, since time is indeed an artificial – nonetheless useful – construct, created by humanity.

When you look out of your home and see people running in the streets in blind rages, destroying both property and themselves, you will know the beginning of the end is already upon you. When you look out of your home and you see people starving on the streets with no place to live you will know the beginning of the end is already upon you.

When you look out of your home and you see multitudes across the planet rioting as nations due to the massive crimes and assaults on the people by their own governments, you will know the end of the tribulations is upon you.

When you look within your own heart and soul and you cry for the pain and suffering humanity has endured you will know you are closer to the end than you realize. When you look within your own heart and soul and you feel compassion for those around you who are suffering, and when you can see them as human beings worthy of respect and care, you will have crossed a very important line in the evolution of humanity.

When you can look outside of yourself and see others as you, you will have evolved into beings of higher consciousness...then you will have made the next step in your progression as a race of beings.

Not everyone will make it. Not everyone will want to. Many will choose to give up along the way, but no soul will be criticized or lost in the transition.

For those of you who choose to stay and endure the entirety of the tribulation period you will witness much suffering, begging and pleading by people of all walks of life. You will see neighbor turn against neighbor before things turn around. You will see famine and drought, war and thunder; you will see natural disasters and not-so-natural disasters.

You can "cushion" yourself and those you love by continually putting a light of protection around yourself, those you love, and your possessions. Not all of the time during the tribulation will be full of sorrow and heartbreak. There will be lighter moments and times, but these will be experienced only by those of you who have not become too wrapped up in the destruction of the world and its systems that will occur all around. This is a time to be self-sufficient and to disengage from society. This is a time to rely upon yourself for guidance and to go within to seek counsel and protection.

The end is not near but the beginning of the end is.

28

Choose the Truth

THE MOMENT FOR TRUTH has come about. The moment for spiritual enlightenment has come about. The moment for all beings to stand up and make a choice has come about. The time is now and the place is here – Earth. There is no more time to fluff about, following this distraction or that distraction. The time has come to settle down and to make a choice to move forward as a race, or to stay where you are and bear the consequences. Humanity now has to make its choice.

In the overall scheme of things, the choice is already quite apparent, but for you who live in the three-dimensional reality of Earth the choice seems to be millions of miles away. Many beings on Earth will choose to evolve as a group rather than stay stagnant.

However, there are some growing pains which must first be endured before you will be able to see the end of the tunnel of darkness and despair. The darkness and despair will serve to move you along more quickly on your path of evolution and development. The darkness and despair will serve as a reminder of what you are working toward – a life and existence that does not contain moments of depression and despondency. A life full of hope, promise and optimism is yours for the asking, but certain steps must first be taken.

First, you must want happiness and joy and not suffering and hardship. Many people find joy in hardship but this is not true joy. This is a misdirected version of the truth – one in which the person who has these feelings suffers from many ailments of the mind and body.

29

A Time to Be Joyful

THIS IS A TIME TO BE JOYFUL – not saddened or downtrodden. The end is not near but the beginning is. This is a reason to celebrate and feel joy in your soul. Your soul, each of your souls, is already rejoicing because it knows the time for resolution and correction of the ills and wrongs of society is at hand. The negative thoughts and emotions that have carried your society forward for eons will now come to an end. Yes, they will come to an end. And yes, it is possible to have a world in which people care about the wellbeing of their fellow human beings. It is possible to have a world in which there is kindness, love, peace, harmony and balance among all individuals and toward all individuals.

How do we get there and when will we get there? We get there by holding tight to the light, by being grounded and present, and trying every minute of every day to abide by the light and its teachings. Look first to yourself and see what changes you can make within yourself. Then look toward others, knowing you cannot control their actions but you are responsible for controlling your reactions. When you have learned to sufficiently control your own thoughts, actions and reactions, you will be ready to move forward on the evolutionary scale of humanity.

In the coming months you will begin to see a difference in humanity on a large scale. You will see people pulling out their hair in anguish. You will see people running to and fro in confusion and madness. You will see people taking their own lives in despair over the economic events that are about to unfold. But fear not, for the guiding principle of life and its creation is always with you and will never desert you. It is not the creative force that has deserted man; rather it is man who has deserted the creative force. Man has forgotten how to be creative. Man has forgotten how to think for itself and to organize his/her life for himself/herself. Man has forgotten how to live life according to his/her own principles and beliefs. There are many roads to the ultimate creative force, but you must choose the one that suits your taste and temperament. Always look within your own heart when someone tells you how you should behave, what is right or wrong, and how you should treat others. Look within your own heart and think about what this person has told you. Analyze what they have told you, think about it from all perspectives, exhaust yourself thinking about it. And when you have done this ask yourself if what they have said sits well with you. Ask yourself if what they have said rings true to your ears and heart. If it does, incorporate their thoughts into your daily practice and into your routine. However, if it does not, you must reject what they have said regardless of the consequences.

To know another's heart, do not listen to their words but watch their actions, for actions do indeed speak louder than words. By a man's actions you will know his heart. Watch how a man treats the poorest and weakest among you, and then you will understand and know the purity of his heart. Never trust a man who is unkind to the poorest individual, for if they treat such a person with contempt and disdain, one day they will treat you in the same manner. It is inevitable because such a person holds himself/herself in disdain and loathing.

How do you treat the lowest among you? Do you treat them with respect and compassion, or do you look down upon them and say it is their own fault? Do you treat them with kindness or do you ignore them and hope they will just go away? This is the standard by which you can assess yourself as well as others. In the coming times of troubles you must be able to discern which individuals are telling you the truth and which are lying to you, because your life may very well depend on it.

Over the next few years many changes will occur both in society and within people's hearts. Many people will become so angry with the government and corporations they will dedicate their lives to the downfall of these organizations. Others will become so desperate and greedy they will seek to steal whatever you have and they will use any means necessary to achieve their aims. These robbers will be on the street, in the government and in boardrooms. In the times to come one must question everything, especially people in positions of power and authority.

However, these times will soon come to an end and when they do you will see a new standard has been set for society. The new standard will be one in which people will have learned to cooperate and work together for a common goal in order to survive. They will now see the link between their own thoughts and actions, and the thoughts and actions of others. People will now begin to understand the power of their own thoughts and actions, and will give more attention to actively creating a better, healthier and more abundant living space for all of humanity. People will have grown tired of the endless cycles of destruction and suffering, and will begin to understand they alone are responsible for these conditions and circumstances.

30

Exercise Your Mind and
Liberate Your Soul

Most of us exist elsewhere on other planets and in other dimensions. The Earth is known as a resting place, an in-between existence place if you will. The purpose of Earth and all the creatures and life forms upon it is to show the way to those on other planets and in other dimensions who have lost their way, and lost their understanding of their place in the universe. The Earth and life upon it serves as a reminder of where we have all come from, and what can happen if laziness and insecurity are allowed to creep into our psyches.

Earth serves as a reminder of all we can be and all we should be. It serves as a remedial course in existence. It is, as you will have noticed, a bit of a crash course in the laws of the universe and in existence on a higher and more profound level.

The events and emotions you experience on Earth are a reminder of the feelings that exist in the universe and the dangers if these emotions are allowed to exist without controls or checks – in other words, with a lack of awareness of their power to create as well as destroy all living organisms. These unchecked emotions destroy life both in a physical sense as well as on an etheric level. All of existence is bound up in the microcosm of life. It is reflected in every action you take and in every thought you have. This is the true meaning and understanding of life…that you are not only what you eat, but also what you think and what you feel. The meaning of life is to be able to connect your thoughts and actions in such a way that you bring joy and peace to yourself, as well as the planet and all life forms on the planet. Once you have accomplished this, you will be able to move on to another realm of existence – one in which there will be no need for remedial classes in existence and the meaning of life, because you will have already attained all knowledge and all understanding.

How do we get there? By not being afraid to push the boundaries of our existence or of our understanding. The more you exercise your mind and liberate your soul the closer you will be to a full and complete understanding of this life, the universe and meaning of eternity and life within all realms.

Don't be afraid to say, "I do not understand". Do not be afraid to encounter concepts that are unfamiliar to you. Do not be afraid to embrace the truth that resonates deep within your core, even if you know those around you will most assuredly think you are crazy. Do not be afraid of what others around you think. Follow your own heart in all things, and by this you will know the truth and understand life in all its abundance and joy.

The truth comes easily to those who willingly and freely open their hearts to the joy of life and all its blessings. Reach out and embrace life and all its facets and you will know reality. Do not sit back and allow life to go on all around you. Step fully into life and you will see the wonders of the planet and of existence on this level. It is not that life on Planet Earth is full of sorrow and hardship. No, it is more that life on Planet Earth is full of rich experiences to be savored and enjoyed. Nowhere else in this universe can you experience such a wide range of emotions and actions. It is like riding a wild roller coaster every day – there is danger and a sense of exhilaration. Those of you lucky enough to be on Planet Earth know extreme highs and extreme lows. However, the "high" you experience when you have conquered the raw and negative emotions of hatred, greed, and self-absorption are like none found anywhere else.

Those of you on Planet Earth are not of the lower classes of the universe but high enough that you have been trusted to pass through Planet Earth, knowing that eventually you will be able to master the feelings of jealousy and hatred, of self-denial and greed, and come out the other side a more compassionate and peaceful being. This is the aim of life on Planet Earth – to achieve a greater awareness and a greater understanding of the universe and the laws that drive it. Actions and thoughts on Planet Earth have an immediate consequence that is not found on other planets or in many of the other dimensions. The consequences of your actions and thoughts while on Planet Earth echo throughout the universe in ways you can only just now begin to imagine, and this is the purpose of life forms on Planet Earth.

31

Live Life Fully

LIFE FORCE HAS MEANING and it serves a purpose. The meaning of life force is to expound upon the glories of creation and to attain a higher state of being in this existence. The purpose of life force is to show you and all of humanity how to live a life more fully so you will understand the complexities of life.

Humanity has managed to remove and shield itself from the complexities of life. We are all living in hermetically sealed jars that are watered-down versions of life, so when an event that is not sanitized comes our way we shudder and turn our faces away in either fear or disgust. This is not what is supposed to happen – not if you want to be a balanced creature fully exploring all that life has to offer.

To fully explore life, we need to face each new situation with grace and dignity. We need to face each new situation with equanimity and peacefulness. We need to understand that this universe, this existence, is about peace and harmony in all situations. We need to understand that none of this is real. It is indeed all an illusion. The illusion of life is meant to teach us things that we would not otherwise be able to learn. By the same token, the experiences here feel real. So, when we are faced with painful decisions and painful situations we need to reach into the depths of our soul and pull out that part which is eternal and all knowing, that part which is still in touch with the universal soul. By reaching out for and consciously asking the universal soul to make its presence and wisdom known, we can face all decisions and situations with a minimum of pain and suffering.

When you reach out and touch your universal soul you are touching all of humanity – all that ever was and all that ever will be. You will find in the universal soul a deep peace and understanding of why you are here and where you are headed.

Many people lose touch with the universal soul when they first feel fear. This is a connection that must be re-established if we are to progress as a race. This does indeed go way beyond the individual. This goes all the way to the universal. Do not get caught up in melodramas and other harsh experiences in this life. Know that whatever comes your way is your chance to learn and move forward without succumbing to the lower forces and vibrations that are also a part of your world. Let go of negativity and free yourself from fear and worry. Attach yourself to the universal soul and you will spread your wings and fly higher and farther than you ever dreamed possible.

You attach yourself to the universal soul by stating firmly in your mind that this is your intention and the rest will take care of itself.

There are no tests or lessons in this world. All negativity is a result of humans attaching their soul to lower vibratory rates and negative emotions, and then being too afraid or too lazy to relinquish them. All suffering is our own individual fault. Nothing can harm a person but that which that person lets harm him or her. You are the keeper of your soul so you decide how you want to live on this planet. Do you want a life of sorrow and misery, or do you want a life of enlightenment and fulfillment? If you want a life of enlightenment and fulfillment, reach out for the universal soul and declare that it is your intention to be a part of the universal soul and to live by the rules and laws established by the universal soul. If you will do this and have faith in your convictions, you will never again feel sorrow or grief.

32

Change

THE KEY TO A HAPPY, JOYFUL LIFE is to let the emotions and events wash over you like a gentle tide of water.

Do not get caught up in time and the passage of time. View each new day and each new experience as an opportunity for fulfillment and joy. There is indeed joy to be found in every one of life's moments...those that are considered good and those that are considered bad. When you can find joy and pleasure in life's most excruciatingly painful experiences, you will know you have achieved full enlightenment. Then you will know you have attained Christhood. Most of us on this plane will never reach this level. It is not because it is unattainable. Rather, most of us do not wish to see the joy in life's painful moments. We would rather wallow in self-pity and victimization than feel true joy.

To feel true joy one must open one's heart fully, and once you do this all sorts of experiences and emotions will come into and through you. That is the key; let the emotions flow through you without distorting your true self. This is how you live up to your full potential. Once you open yourself up fully you will begin to see the very foundation of creation – how the universe came to exist and why it exists. Do not try to understand with your mind because once you step onto that road you will have already lost the battle. Just feel, nothing more, nothing less. You do not have to become a vegetarian, you do not have to meditate 12 hours a day, you do not have to walk barefoot to holy sites of pilgrimage. No, all you have to do is feel your emotions – all of them – and let them wash over you just as a free-flowing river moves downstream.

Embrace change and do not resist change. Most of us are afraid of change...we resist change with all our might because we think or we fear it will take something away from us and will bring us something bad. This is not the case. All of life is based on change. Every day millions of cells in your body die off and are replaced with new ones. Change is inevitable. Change is what makes life glorious and fun. Change makes life an adventure, as long as you remember to let the events and emotions brought about by change wash over you and pass through you. Do not hold on to what once was. Do not think your life last year was so much better than it is this year. Do not waste your time wondering why certain people have said certain things to you. That is the past and the past is nothing but a reflection of what has changed. With each change comes the chance to have new experiences and to see the world from a different perspective. As we gain experiences in life our perception alters. If nothing ever changed we would be trapped in limbo – a situation that would offer no enlightenment or chance for growth and experience beyond our own narrow realm of comprehension.

Change is why we are here. Change is what brings us life and joy. How boring would it be to go to the same office, see the same people, eat the same food and have the same conversation day after day after day? Change is what adds the spice to life and gives us enjoyment and pleasure. So you see, change should be embraced and not shunned or resisted. Without change you would be miserable!

So, the key to a successful and pleasurable life is to embrace change while letting the emotions and events pass through you so you are left with the experience and knowledge of every moment, but are free of the residue of holding onto negative emotions and thoughts. Resistance to change creates the same stumbling blocks to joy as does holding on to negative emotions. All is not lost if tomorrow you lose your job. While this type of dramatic change can be frightening, know that God and the angels are always there to guide you in the right direction and to ensure that whatever you experience will be for your highest good and not to your detriment. Change becomes to your detriment when you wish for what was and are afraid to move forward in the stream of life. Just like a blocked river cannot flow freely, neither can you and your life flow freely if you resist change or hold on to what once was, or try to create what will be in the future. Do not try to create your future. Life is a delicate balance that few, if any, of us on this plane fully comprehend. Therefore, let go and just watch what life brings. Life is a play and the Earth is a stage. Enjoy your time here and be open to change and whatever life throws your way. This is the secret of life.

33

Unlock the Journey of Your Soul

THE END IS NOT NEAR, but the future is. The future of humanity is upon you all and it is changing every day. No, the future is not written in stone...more like it is written in sand, at least most of it anyway. There are certain large events and catastrophes scheduled to take place and these cannot be stopped. However, there are multitudes of other events and happenings that do not have to occur. These are the ones of which we speak when we say not everything is written in stone.

What are these events and happenings? These are events and happenings that relate to people's personal safety and wellbeing. You do not have to suffer and neither does anyone else in the human race. The suffering part is really up to you. If you want to suffer, if you feel you need to suffer, you will suffer. However, if you do not want to suffer or you do not feel the need to suffer, you will not. Yep, it is just that simple, direct and easy.

So how do you avoid suffering with what is coming up? There will still be a lot of people who choose suffering over grace but that is their decision. If you want to avoid suffering in the upcoming trials and tribulations, read on. If you do not want to avoid suffering put this book down now and walk away. There is no criticism involved if you want to suffer. We all have our own plots and reasons in this life and a path of no suffering is not for everyone...although this will be hard to understand once the suffering really kicks in and starts in earnest.

What is coming your way, humanity? A force of nature unlike any you have ever seen is one thing. Another thing is devastation and destruction unlike you have ever seen. Remember, the end is not near but the future is. You are about to embark on a journey of the soul...all of you are. There is no way around this. The time has come for humanity to put up or shut up when it comes to consciousness and its evolution. The way forward will be made clear for those of you who wish to move forward at the current pace and scale of development. For those of you who do not wish to move forward time will simply cease to exist or stop if you will. For some of you the end is near. In fact, for a great number of you the end is imminent. The end for the vast majority of humans will come as a result of a massive cataclysm in the sky. This cataclysm will wipe out all plants, animals and humans. This type of cataclysm has occurred before in your human history and will undoubtedly occur again in the distant future.

However, not all of you are ready to give up and start over. Some of you are ready to move forward on the scale of evolution. Some of you are ready to take the next leap of development and embrace the world as it really is. Some of you are ready to see the truth about your existence and the meaning of that existence. We will get to more about that in a moment but first let us digress to make one point very clear. We are not here to show you what you should do. We are not here to point you in the right direction. That we cannot do. The only thing we can do is open up certain avenues of reality and existence. What you choose to do with these avenues and what directions you go in from there is up to you, and those of humanity who are left on this planet. The future is in no way set in stone, so we can only show you the doors that are available; what you do with those areas once the doors have been opened is up to you. We do not know how you will proceed and we do not know what kind of future you will make for yourselves. The only thing we do know at this point is that a fair amount of you will decide to take the plunge and see what is on the other side of some of these doors. And for this we applaud your courage and your stamina, because to get to this point of development has taken eons for most of you.

Now, on to other matters.

Many of you, about a third of the current human population, will choose to move forward on the evolutionary scale of consciousness. You will choose to open your hearts and minds to all that which is around you and inside of you. Scary thought, huh, that which is inside of you? Don't be frightened and don't be overly concerned. There is nothing bad in there. Only things and abilities which most of you have forgotten you had. You have tucked away inside of you abilities and talents that if you were to display them right now would rock the world on its axis (not literally but figuratively). The day is coming when it will be time to unlock all those hidden abilities and talents. For these are gifts that have been created by you and for you. Now is the time to unleash these powers for the benefit of humanity and the human race. Now is the time to move forward with speed and skill.

You can unlock these powers and gifts by clearing your mind and focusing on your strengths, instead of your weaknesses. Focus on what you want instead of what you do not want. Focus on your goodness and not your badness or wrongness. These are the things you must do if you want to unlock and tap into these wondrous gifts you have given yourself. Do not be afraid to explore the depths of your own mind, heart and soul. There is no big boogey man waiting there to tear you asunder or wipe out your dreams with one swipe. The only thing or person waiting there is you, and do you really want to create chaos in your own life or harm yourself? We do not think so. So open the doors to your unconscious and see what gifts and knowledge you have to reveal to yourself. Nothing is written in stone, remember?

So, if you do not like what you see. If you do not like having the power of these gifts, you can just as easily close the door to your subconscious and never open it again. There is no point of "no return". You always have free will to do and choose what makes you happy for that moment. However, we are now asking some of you to go beyond your current comfort zone. We are asking a lot of you to push the limits of your understanding and to come on a journey with us to the deepest and darkest part of your soul. We do not say "dark" because there is something sinister there. Rather, we say "dark" because it is a part of your soul that has been locked away tightly for eons.

Now is the time to open up your soul and see what lies beneath the façade of human existence. Now is the time to open up your heart and see what true unconditional love feels like. Now is the time to see the world around you with new eyes of comprehension and understanding. Now is the time to let go of the shackles that have held you down as a people, as a group. Now is the time to break free of self-imposed limitations and restrictions. Now is the time to set your soul free and see where you can go. Soar higher than your wildest dreams and plant your feet firmly in a new reality – a reality freer and more liberating than anything you have ever seen. It is time to come to a new reality where there is no more pain and suffering. We know this is a hard concept for you to grasp, but please believe us when we tell you this kind of three-dimensional world is possible and it is attainable for all of you, if you will just let go of your antiquated ideas of what is right and wrong, possible and impossible.

The new world and reality that awaits you is one of glorious rapture and being. It is a place of merriment and joy. It is a place where the lamb will lay down with the lion. Do a lot of these descriptions sound familiar? They should. We have planted these concepts into the hearts and minds of generations of humans from all races and walks of life. There is a reason, of course. We wanted you to know deep in your soul that this kind of existence was possible and was just around the corner, eventually. We wanted you to know your full potential…what you were really capable of achieving.

Now the time has come to explore this new reality. See if it is something you really want to move toward. Not everyone will feel they are ready to step into this new reality. Not everyone will be willing to give up the feelings and emotions you currently experience on a minute-by-minute basis. Some of you will decide to stay in the current form of existence and start the world and cycle over yet again. And there is nothing wrong with this decision. It is where you are on the evolutionary scale at this moment. It is not "better" to choose to jump forward on the evolutionary scale at this moment…it is just a different form of existence you are choosing now. Eons from now you will be faced with yet another decision. To jump forward or to stay where you are and start all over again. This is how time works.

Time is indeed an artificial construct invented by sentient beings on Earth. However, time serves a purpose too. Time serves the purpose of helping humanity order its thoughts and classify its time periods at a fundamental level, so humanity can then decide on a superficial level that they have spent long enough here at this current stage of development and are ready to move forward. Once you move forward you will encounter a new form of linear time that will not be so linear, but will also serve the purpose of helping you to order your thoughts and decide when is the right time to move forward…and so the cycle will continue until you reach your final destination, which will be a complete reunification with All That Is and All That Will Ever Be. Big words, huh? Big concepts, huh?

Your mind is not so undeveloped and small that it cannot grasp what is being said here. Now is the time to push the envelope and to think about concepts and ideas which you have never thought of before. We told you, now is the time to move forward and breathe in the air of expansion and limitless possibilities. Now is the time to open your hearts and minds and see what lies ahead.

34

Understanding Happiness

HAPPINESS IS AN ART FORM – one of maturity and wit, calmness and suffering. We say suffering because that is what everyone thinks must occur for there to be happiness – sort of like a dual band and opposites attract. This is not the case. There does not have to be suffering in order to have happiness. You do not need to first experience suffering so that you can have something with which to compare happiness. Happiness is a state of mind; a state of being that comes from deep within you. It is not something that can be generated by personal achievements or accomplishments. It is something that just is. It is a part of who you are. Likewise, it is not something that can be taken from you. Happiness is at your core and everyone's core. Whether or not you choose to let it out, to experience it, is another matter and one that is totally up to the individual.

Happiness cannot be bought nor can it be explained. It is something which just is…like the joy in your heart when you see a puppy frolicking on unstable legs, when you see a bird flying free in the air, when you see a kitten rolling in the grass reveling in nature's bounty. These are moments of true happiness and they cannot be manufactured or bought. They are a part of your essence and being, just as being alive is a part of your essence and being. Life is a miracle of nature and cannot be bought. Life is the coming together of certain energies in a certain way that combine to create what you call life. If one of those elements is missing, the equation does not add up to life. The same can be said for humanity. If one of the parts is missing, the equation will not add up to survival and expansion. Yes, we keep coming back to this point because there is much you must understand in a relatively short period of time.

The end is not near but the future is. We keep repeating this phrase because we want you to understand that many of you will survive and go on to flourish. However, many will not and it is in watching the death and destruction of the many that will not survive that you will begin to lose your resolve, and will begin to show fear and make decisions that might be irrational. That's okay, we understand the pressure that will be on your shoulders and we want you to know we are all there to help you every minute, through every circumstance. At this point no action or event in your life is random. All events now have greater significance than ever before. You are on the road to salvation and you will see the Promised Land. The Promised Land is not a physical locality. Rather it is a state of mind, a state of mind achievable through grace and perseverance. Not all of you who pass on to the next dimension will have the same level of understanding or grace.

The future is now. The time for the next dimension to reveal itself is now. Before this happens fully though there are certain events which must transpire on this planet. One of those events is a great earthquake which will strike every continent. The earthquake will shake the very foundation of humanity because of its magnitude and destructiveness. No continent will be unscathed when the earthquake occurs. There will actually be a series of earthquakes that will cause humanity to think the Earth will never stop shaking. However, while on the surface it will seem that there are a series of massive earthquakes, this is not the case. In actuality, there will be one massive tremor or shake that will radiate up from the Earth's core, striking different areas at slightly different times due to lag time and distance from the Earth's core to the surface.

Now, this series of earthquakes, or so it will seem to you, will cause complete havoc and panic in many countries. Those countries who are hit with the quake will wish they had never been, so great will be the suffering of its people. Those countries who are not hit by the quake will live in fear and trepidation that their country will be next. As a rule of thumb, the quake will hit those countries that are most in need of making a shift to the new way of thinking, and being – to the new consciousness. While it may look like those countries that are hit have been singled out for great destruction, this is not the case. Those countries that will be hit are greatly blessed because they will be given the opportunity to change their ways overnight, so great will the destruction be. Everything they have known will disintegrate in the blink of an eye. They will have no choice but to rebuild and start anew. By starting anew they have the chance to get it right this time in terms of moving ahead on the evolutionary scale of consciousness.

Not all countries that will be destroyed will choose to move ahead on the evolutionary scale of consciousness...we know that...but enough will.

Another event that will occur is that of floods. Water will sweep across the plateaus and ravines of Western Europe, Eastern Europe and the Middle East. Yes, the Middle East. Places that have never had floods will experience floods, and places that have never known heat will know scorching heat. These reverse actions of nature will come about as a result of a catastrophe in space. An explosion of an interplanetary star will set off a chain reaction of events that man will be helpless to stop or contain. The only thing man will be able to do is to hunker down and wait for the worst of it to pass. This will take two to three years in total and will wipe out large segments of life on Earth. The massive explosion itself will occur in the next one to two years.

The scorching heat will bring wildfires to many regions and will pollute the atmosphere for years. All will not be doom and despair though. These disasters will be a wake-up call for much of humanity, and with this wake-up call will come a new attitude among people, an attitude of coming together for survival instead of the prevailing "each man for himself" attitude that characterizes your planet today. In the face of these natural catastrophes there will be no one to blame. People will have to come together and work together for their common good and for survival. This action will help usher in a new existence on Earth…one of co-existence and mutual trust. No longer will we hear people shout, "Go away or I will shoot!"; no longer will we hear people arguing about whose car banged into whom. Instead, we will hear shouts of joy and laughter that come from hearts filled with happiness and joy. Remember, happiness is a state of being that is independent of the circumstances that may surround you. If you are happy in your heart, that joy will always be with you no matter what. This is why we started this section with happiness.

35

You Have Nothing to Fear

THE TIME HAS COME for humanity to decide which way it wants to proceed. One can either give up right now, or one can proceed along the path to enlightenment and a new beginning. The way is clear for all those who are listening. Again we say there does not have to be suffering on this planet. Man does not have to sit idly by and watch his neighbor die. No, man can step up now and do what is in everyone's best interest and that is to start working on yourself, your inner being, your inner light. Let the wisdom inside each and every one of you come out. Use this wisdom to create a better environment and a better future for yourself and others. There is no ending to this story. Hopefully, enough of you will decide to carry the torch of enlightenment and proceed on to the next plane of existence, which will be everything you ever dreamed it would be and more.

There is a place in your existence that is indeed the Garden of Eden. It is still right here on Earth but it is in a different dimension than the one most of you now inhabit. The Garden of Eden did not disappear. It just became shielded from man's sight because humanity became foul and obsessed with their own profit and gain. We have now come full circle to a time wherein the Garden of Eden is available to those of you who want to go there. The path to the Garden will not always be easy. You will see many tragedies along the way. We are not making it hard for you. You are making it hard for yourself. You must let go of your childish attachments to fear and greed if you want to ascend to the Garden of Eden, to enter the next dimension. The only one who can hold you back is you. The Garden is open to all but not all will be able to see it. For those of you fortunate enough to see it your eyes will be dazzled by its color and beauty. Never in your lives, in any lifetime, have you seen such beauty or felt such peace and tranquility.

The way ahead is clear for a great many of you. The way ahead is fraught with dangers for a great many of you. And the way ahead is non-existent for a great number of you.

For those of you who wish to proceed along the evolutionary path and enter the Garden of Eden, the way will be made even clearer as time goes on. You will be shown in exact detail what you need to do in order to cast off the blinders that that have blocked your sight. You will be shown how to breathe and even how to walk in order to communicate more fully with the living being you know as Planet Earth. You will learn to walk in harmony with the great Planet Earth. You will no longer struggle against the universe or fail to heed its call. You will be one with the universe and the Universal Consciousness.

Look into your heart – what do you see? If you see hatred, lust and greed, you can be sure your end will come soon. If, when you look into your heart, you see kindness and compassion, you still have a chance. If, when you look into your heart, you see white and silver, you know you have no shadows lurking that will create pain and suffering for you in the times to come. You know you have nothing to fear, not even yourself. Throw doubt to the wind and live life to its fullest right now and for the next few years. Do not get bogged down in the details of daily life. Rather, keep your eye on the prize, so to speak, and remember why you are here on Earth at this time – to proceed to the next level of conscious development. Believe it or not, there are many more levels after this one, but we will leave that story for another place and time.

Open your eyes now and see the world around you for what it is – a farce. The worries and concerns people are so caught up in are meaningless. They have no intrinsic value and offer no solace to anyone, quite the opposite actually. These cares and worries serve to drag man down, to dampen your spirit and to hold you back. Let go of the petty concerns and worries and you will soon find yourself flying free from all attachments. Do not worry about your job or how much money you have in the bank. All will be taken care of as long as you remember to let go of your cares and worries and just trust the universe and its infinite wisdom and understanding. Remember, we do not create suffering – you do. So ask yourself what you are doing differently than we are – worrying! Remove fear, doubt and worry from your life and we promise you will see a new you and have a new beginning. We understand not all of you will be able to just magically stop worrying. We understand not all of you will be able to just magically lose your attachment to money and power. We are not asking you to become perfect overnight. All we are saying is make an attempt...try. That is all you have to do in order to proceed to the next level of being. Make an effort and you will be rewarded beyond your wildest dreams. Make an effort and see what new direction your life and thoughts go in. Just make an attempt to do what is right and you will survive the upcoming holocaust.

36

The Universe Will Guide You

To CROSS OVER into the other dimension is not meant to be difficult; the only reason the time before the crossing will be difficult is because of humanity and its vain attempts to control the world and its atmosphere. There will always be things you do not understand. The appropriate course of action would therefore be to proceed with caution and not "just do something, anything" in the hope that it will stop whatever is coming. The universe consists of a very delicate balance affected by thoughts, words and actions. All of these have an impact on your world and your psyche. Hold on to positive thoughts, listen for what the universe has to say to you and then proceed. This is where man has so often gone awry. Man attempts to "correct" a situation he knows nothing about and then there is a causal reaction, usually unanticipated. Whereas if man had stopped when confronted with the dilemma and sought guidance from the universe, the way forward would have been made clear and the initial problem would not have been compounded and spun out of control. Spinning out of control is a good way to describe man on Earth now.

People are reaching for whatever they think will make them happy. Man will do whatever it takes to be successful in the eyes of his peers. Man will forfeit his life if he thinks it will buy him/her one more ounce of safety and security. These are all the wrong reactions. They are wrong in that these reactions create more hardship and pain in the long run. This is part of the reason why there will be so many disasters coming up in the near future. They are warning signs to those who have ears to hear and eyes to see. They are a massive wake-up call to those who have the will to see. Take heed of the wake-up call and begin to work on your inner being.

Don't panic and don't cry out to a nameless God in the heavens. Look inward and see what you can do to change your world. Monitor your thoughts and watch your actions and reactions closely. Always stop and ask yourself whether your action or reaction is that of a person operating in complete trust and faith that the universe wishes them no harm, or if it is the action or reaction of a person trapped in fear and panic. Stop, slow down and go inward before making big decisions. The universe will always be there to guide you. The universe will never forsake you. The universe will give you the peace, calmness and balance you need to survive the upcoming disasters. The universe wants your complete happiness and wellbeing. You are the ones who stand in the way of this state of being. It is now time to remove the cloak that has surrounded humanity for eons. It is now time to step out into the world as it was meant to be. It is now time to experience life as it was meant to be lived – not in some dark hole or cave in the side of a mountain, but in full view of all around you. Take the next step and see the world as it really is – a ball of shining light bringing peace, harmony and tranquility. You do not have to be a saint to step into the next dimension. You only have to be ready for change and to have made an effort to enlighten yourself.

To survive unharmed in the face of the upcoming disasters is possible. In fact, it is more than possible – it is what we want for all of you. As we have said before, many of you will choose not to proceed and will therefore start over. That is fine because eventually you will make the leap into the next dimension. It will just take a while longer. The universe and time within the universe is eternal, so whether you succeed in stepping into the next dimension today, tomorrow or four hundred millennia from now really doesn't matter. You will all get there in the end (but not the end of time and existence). Our focus in writing this book at this time is to help those of you who are ready, able and willing to step into the next dimension. We are here to help you now.

III. One Person Can Make a Difference

37

Work on Your Inner Core

THE EFFORTS OF THE MANY will not confound the efforts of the few. The few are those of you who wish to proceed to the next dimension. The efforts of the many will be wasted in vain attempts to bring some reason and order to their rapidly diminishing world. The efforts of the few will not be wasted. Their efforts will be rewarded with a new life and new existence in the very near future. There is no reason to worry, panic or blame anyone else, because we all have our own thoughts, patterns and actions for which we are responsible. These thoughts and actions are what make us human and give us a sense of accomplishment and desire – the desire to achieve what we previously thought was impossible. To achieve what we previously thought was insurmountable. No obstacle is so big as to be insurmountable. All tragedies and events can and will be overcome in a positive and healthy way by those few of you who hold fast to the truth in your hearts. Those few of you who will choose to step into the next dimension will do so at a rapid rate and almost without effort (the actual transition part). The effort you had to expend to get to that point may be no small matter, but we will get to more of that later. Right now we want to discuss what the final days will bring, and what they will look like, and what you should do to prepare for that moment.

First of all, you should all work on your inner being, the core of your existence. Why is this so important you might ask? Well, your inner being is the sum of all you are and all you can be. Your inner core is what makes you human. It is also what makes you so alive and vibrant. All humans are alive and vibrant but not all shine with the luminosity of which they are capable. This is the key. You must work to shine with the luminosity that is possible within your makeup. Do not worry about eating meat or not eating meat. This is not about anything that is on the outside of you. This discussion concerns only what is inside of you. You all need to work on reaching in and touching your inner core. Many, if not most, of you will have no idea how to do that, for it has been so long since you have been in touch with that part of yourself.

The method is easy and straightforward. Sit quietly in a room without distraction or noise. Listen to your breath and watch it move in and out of your nostrils. Focus on your heart area and just be. Feel what is there. See what is there and feel what is there. This is the first step in acknowledging and getting in touch with your inner core.

After you have been doing this for a while, maybe five minutes or so, pay attention to your breath. Is your breath rate and quality different than it was when you began? When your breath rate slows and becomes even and steady you are ready to move on to the second step in this process.

With your eyes closed, take an inventory of what you want in life and from life. Think about things that happened years ago and think about things that happened yesterday. Think about things that make you sad and make you happy. Think about things that make you angry and those that make you joyful…but don't stop thinking, not at this point. Feel the emotions rush through your mind and your body. Feel the full weight and impact these emotions have on your system and on your breathing. Once you have done this for several minutes stop all thoughts and just relax with your eyes closed.

Now, take your right hand and place it on your left shoulder. Sit with your right hand on your left shoulder for several minutes – thinking of nothing if possible.

Put your right hand back down on your lap – it does not matter which way the palm is facing.

Take your shoulders and pull them away from your ears and pull them back so your spine is tall and straight. Feel the energy that has been released as it crawls up your spine and into your crown chakra. Feel the direct connection with the universe. Feel your inner core begin to open up and connect once again with the Universal Consciousness and all that is out there. Feel your body as it comes alive and shines from within. Breathe in as deeply as possible a few times and then settle back into a regular breathing pattern. Let go of your fears and worries. Let go of anything you feel might be keeping you in this dimension. Let go and feel the freedom it brings. Let go and let your mind and body wander into the depths of your soul previously closed off to you and your senses. Let go and breathe in the air of freedom and possibility.

Do this exercise two to three times per week at first. As you become more and more comfortable with it and its effect, you will only need to do this exercise once or twice a week and eventually you will not need to do it at all, because you will have succeeded in putting all cares and thoughts away and will be living totally within yourself and with your inner being.

You see, we said it would not be difficult. There is no great strain involved.

When you first start doing these exercises you might find that certain patterns of thoughts and behaviors will begin to change – to remedy themselves. You will find you will be more outgoing because you will have less fear about what others might say or do. You may find you breathe more easily and more deeply all the time. You will feel a difference, no matter how small or insignificant it may seem at first. But these differences will mark a new beginning in your life. They will mark the time when you first began to live within yourself and within your inner being.

The time will shortly come when you will need to do these exercises more frequently to keep your mind clear of the traumas existing around you. Many people will be killed and many people will die in the upcoming years, but as we have said before this is what they have chosen and it is the best path for them given their current frame of mind. Again, do not pity or judge those who will die. Graciously accept that is their will and it has nothing to do with you or your future on this planet. Your only concern at this point in time is to work on your inner being and to become the shining being of light of which you are capable.

The time will come soon when men will wrack their brains trying to find a solution to their economic and catastrophic problems. Do not let the solutions to these problems trouble you or concern you, because you will not be waiting around for the result. You will be off with those like-minded people who have decided to cross over into the next dimension. Your world will instantly become stable and ordered. Your world will instantly become harmonious and peaceful. Your world will become that which is created by your inner being, your inner core.

38

Don't Give Up

THE COMING EVENTS and dislocations will be the result of errant behavior as far as the norms of the universe are concerned. Meaning, it is man's rejection of living in harmony with itself, nature and the universe that will create so much heartbreak and bloodshed. Man is not being punished for his errant behavior. Rather, he has made the situation far more difficult and painful than it has to be to get to the next level. As we have said before, some have chosen this way of ending, while others will just be carried away by the strong tide of events. There are still others among you who will know what the right course is and will follow it. And by following it they will arrive safely on the next level of evolution.

We keep making this point because we want to make sure you understand there will be three groups of people from here – those who are listening to the call of the universe, those who are absolutely not listening and who have no intention of listening, and those poor souls who through the lack of any strong beliefs or principles will just be carried away in the stream of devastation and destruction that will afflict your planet soon.

Be watchful and seek out those who slot into the same category as you. From them you will gain strength, knowledge and a greater understanding in the times to come. At this point, do not waste your time being around those who do not have the same goal as you do – that of moving to the next level of understanding. By the same token, do not judge or look down upon those who have chosen not to move to the next level at this time. Understand they have reasons you may never understand, yet they are valid for them at this point in time. Focus on yourself and your growth at this time and not on the perceived failings of others. Focus on your goodness and lightness and this will keep you away from much of the destruction and despair that is coming up.

This devastation and destruction of which we speak will be in the form of natural and manmade calamities. Neither is better or worse than the other in the grand scheme of things. All the upcoming calamities will serve a purpose and are not the actions of an angry God or universe punishing humanity for its errant ways. You have brought them upon yourself and you will have to find your way out of them.

For those of you who desire to move to the next level, don't give up. Stay centered and calm. Stay within yourself and you will see that the winds of devastation will pass you by. The events that will happen offer an unprecedented opportunity for some of you to find true peace of mind, body and spirit.

39

The Universe Is
Unconditional Love

Do not let fear of the unknown or fear of dying cloud your judgment in the days to come. Do not let the weight of indecision carry you down the path of ruin and destruction in the days to come. There is a way open to all to avoid pain and bloodshed. There is a way open to all that will resonate with love and harmony. Open your eyes and see the world for what it is – a collection of thoughts and energy, nothing more and nothing less. Depersonalize the world and you will see it for what it is. Remove your ego from the equation that everything revolves around you personally and is happening to you personally, and you will fare much better in the times to come. The times to come will be filled with agony for many of you. The times to come will be filled with heartbreak and judgment for many of you. However, there are those among you who will find their way to the next level without so much as a bump in the road. There are those among you who will find their way to the next level in the blink of an eye. Then there are those among you who will have to work a little harder to get to the next level.

Regardless of which category you find yourself in, know this – you are loved and you are nothing but love. That is the stuff of which the universe is made, absolute unconditional love. How can the universe be made up of unconditional love? It is not matter. It is not substance. It is only an emotion, you say? Well, it is more than just an emotion. Indeed, the universe is built upon the emotion of unconditional love – that is where we all come from, and where we all return when our time on this planet is at an end. The basic building block of the universe is the emotion of unconditional love. Your scientists have proven that your basic structure, your DNA, can be altered and affected by emotions. Why do you think this is? Because emotion is the foundation of the universe and unconditional love is the cornerstone of everything that is.

Sounds incredible, doesn't it? This is why we are asking all of you to get in touch with your inner being, your inner core, as soon as possible. By doing this you will be accessing that part of you which is the cornerstone of the universe's foundation. Re-accessing that part of you will enable you to move through the upcoming times without fear and without trepidation, and when fear is lessened or not present (although few of you will be able to maintain an attitude completely lacking fear) your worries and troubles will diminish in a corresponding fashion. When fear is taken out of the equation, you will be able to see the world and the events for what they really are – warning signs for those of you who still refuse to see and hear. The more people fear, the worse will be the outcome physically, emotionally and psychically.

Start now on reducing your fear levels and trusting in the universe, which is built upon unconditional love, to guide you and protect you in the coming times. The more you connect with this loving universe, the stronger and more able you will be to cope with the coming times and to cross into the next level of consciousness.

You will not suffer if you do not want to. But in order not to suffer you must remove fear and doubt from the equation.

The world is a wondrous place full of light and joy, but only for those who are willing to see it. In the present day and age, this wondrous part of the world does not just come to you. You have to go out and get it. You have to cut through the veil of misunderstanding that has shrouded your planet and your minds for eons. To see through this veil you must return within and re-access your inner core, which is unconditional love and forgiveness. By doing this, you will be able to see the world and the upcoming events for what they are. You will understand the deeper meaning and mysteries of life. You will see a tower of confusion and understand immediately what is really going on and what is really being said, regardless of the words being used. You will look into men's souls and see what they value and what they reject. It is what they *reject* that you need to look at most closely. For what a person *rejects* is that part of himself/herself that she/he is not honoring, that part of life which frightens her/him the most, and that part of being that brings him/her the most fear and hatred.

What a person *accepts* is what makes her/him feel comfortable and safe. What a person *accepts* is not always what is best for that person in the long run though. Many of us accept errant behavior on a daily basis, errant behavior in ourselves and others. We accept it because it is easy and we don't want to create waves. By our acceptance of these behaviors, we don't have to think or look within. If we began to question what was going on around us, we would have to admit we too have been in error. This is precisely what most people do not want to do. They do not want to admit they had a hand in all the devastation and destruction going on around them. They prefer to remain the innocent victim and blame God, politicians, religious leaders and those in charge for what has happened.

But this is not the whole story. By your own thoughts and actions over your lifetimes you have created the scenario we are now witnessing. You are responsible for all that is happening, so stop blaming others. Stop putting out more hatred and fear. Take responsibility and do what you can to minimize the cycle of pain and grief the world is now experiencing. Get in touch with your inner self, your inner being, and re-access your limitless supply of compassion and understanding. Help make the world a better place immediately by putting away your fears and worries and getting in touch with your eternal core, your eternal essence of love.

40

Stay Grounded and Centered

THE ROAD HAS BEEN LONG and winding for some of you, while for others it has been a relatively easy path to where you are today. And when we say, "where you are today", we mean in terms of evolution as individuals and as a group. For some of you, the way will continue to be relatively smooth, while for others the road will get bumpy. The way ahead stretches before each and every one of you, and each and every one of you will have to make a decision quite soon. This decision will be whether you wish to continue on your current path or to get off the bus, so to speak. The way forward is not so clear for many of you who have spent less time developing your spiritual skills. It is these spiritual skills that will help you get through the troubled times ahead.

The spiritual skills will help keep you grounded and centered, and focused on what really matters, and stop you from getting caught up in the hysteria that is to come. It may be hard to believe the world will be rocked by mass hysteria, but it will. The hysteria will follow different events, some natural and some manmade. This hysteria will lead you into fear and darkness. This hysteria will lead you into Hell on Earth. You must each learn to witness the hysteria but not get caught up in it. There will be times when you will say this is easier said than done and we agree. But know we are here to help you every minute of every day. No matter how many times you fall we will be there to pick you up and to help you along your way.

Why is it so important that humanity progress and pass through the coming times of trouble? The existence of many races and planets actually depends on how humanity passes this time. If humanity progresses to the next stage of evolution, many new realms and dimensions will open up for humans, as well as other creatures and beings.

A calm mind and peaceful heart will get you through the hard times ahead. Remember to take a moment each and every day to calm your mind and settle your heart. This should only take a few minutes, but over time it will prove invaluable to your sense of self and your groundedness. Start now by taking a moment each morning to be alone with your thoughts and heartbeat. Hear your heartbeat and focus only on that. This will help you to intuitively recognize what is real and what is make believe. This exercise will also help you gain a better understanding of what it means to live and to die. You will get a better understanding of why you are here, and what can be done to help humanity progress.

41

The Essence of Life Is Eternal

IT IS THE TIME and manner of death that is upsetting – not death itself. Death is the only certain thing in life, and it comes to all of us at one time or another. Death does not matter because there is always life after death, just in another form and at another frequency. The essence of life, the energy of life, does not end and cannot be destroyed. Our essence continues long after our physical bodies have decomposed. It is this essence of life itself that we should celebrate and acknowledge as the true meaning of life. It is this essence of life that we should focus our attention on and pay heed to when we are in a physical body. It is the essence of life that matters, and not what we acquire or what we accomplish on this earthly plane. This is what humanity should focus on and not trivial matters, materialism or false sanctity. The everlasting life essence is what follows us throughout time and space. It is the essence of life that is undeniable and will always remain with us. Therefore, it is better to focus on the essence of life and not on our life on the physical plane. Life on the physical plane is meaningless and temporary.

Your life essence will carry you through to other times and dimensions. It is your life essence that will lead you to the Promised Land, whether on this earthly plane or in the heavenly realms. It is your life essence that needs to be developed and protected, not your earthly possessions. Your life essence is a part of you that will never die and will never abandon you. Therefore, work on your life essence by reaching in and getting in touch with your soul. See what your soul has to say and follow where your soul leads you. Your soul is the only thing that should concern you while you are on this earthly plane.

How does one reach in and get in touch with your soul? You sit quietly and do the meditation described before (in Chapter 40 "Stay Grounded and Centered"). Do this meditation regularly and you will see your perceptions shift. You will see your world around you change, for the better.

Your will see new doors and new avenues open up before you. Do this meditation and you will be in touch with your soul. You will understand why you are here and what purpose you serve. These are the main questions humans ask – why am I here and what purpose does my life serve? This is the fundamental question for humanity, and at one time or another we will all ask this simple yet profound question. It is in asking this question that we open our minds to the possibility that there may be something beyond ourselves and our small lives. It is in asking this question that we begin to see there is something more than ourselves at stake. It is in asking this question that we begin to realize there is a greater purpose to our lives than going to work, having kids and playing in the garden with our pets. It is in asking this question that we begin to question whether there is a God, whether there is a universe beyond our own comprehension.

Asking this question is the first step in understanding the bigger picture, in understanding there is a world, a dimension, that is outside our understanding at this point – that there is more to life and living than what we currently perceive. This is what we are here to show you at this point. We are here to show you the world(s) that exist just outside your current range of perception. However, the time is coming soon when these worlds or dimensions will not be outside the range of many of you. Many of you will soon begin to see these "new" worlds and dimensions, and when you do you will at first be startled by what you see. You will see kindness and considerateness. You will see compassion and true feeling. You will see humanity at its best even as you see humanity at its worst. You will see what is possible for humanity to achieve, even as many around you will be killing their neighbors and friends.

But even as you see these "tragic" events you will know in your heart what is possible for humanity to achieve. You will see the true potential of humanity as we see it. And you will know in your hearts that this is where you want to be and what you want to achieve. You will stay grounded and you will stay aware of all that is around you. There are many among you who already know what humanity is capable of achieving. You may not know it on a conscious level but you know it in your hearts because your *soul* knows it. Those of you who already know on a soul level what humanity is capable of achieving are here on this planet at this time to help humanity as a group along the path of peace, forgiveness and enlightenment. You know what you are doing and why you are here, even if you do not consciously know what you are doing and why you are here.

The time is coming when you will be asked to stand up and help lead humanity along the path of peace, forgiveness and compassion. When the time is right you all will know intuitively what to do and how to behave. There is no great miracle that will take place. There is no great revelation that will occur on a mass scale. There will be a slow trickle of actions and information that will leak out into the world and slowly, or not so slowly, transform the world and the human consciousness.

This is why you all are here – to aid and assist humanity in opening up to a new way of being and a new way of living.

42

Who You Truly Are

THE ENERGY OF NEW DIMENSIONS and new ways of existence are opening up for many of you on the earthly plane. With this new energy will come new challenges and new obstacles. However, the road ahead will not be as difficult as you might fear, because with these new energies comes a heightened sense of awareness of what is going on around you. Those of you who choose to tap into these new energies will be rewarded with renewed vigor and a sense of purpose. The ability to see what is going on around you with a true understanding will be of prime importance, if you are to minimize suffering and heartache for yourself and others.

As the house of cards known as your current financial system begins to collapse in on itself, remember none of this is real. None of this has anything to do with your inner being. The financial system and all its cogs are mere illusions and playthings. These are just constructs humanity has put in place to help themselves along the path of true understanding and wisdom. Sometimes the greatest understanding can come from rejecting a system of thought, as much as from adopting a system of thought. We see many of you rushing around trying to find the answer to life. We see you embracing this belief system and then another belief system, only to end up rejecting this or that thought system because it did not fulfill your expectations, and did not give you true understanding of yourselves or your universe. Then, after time, you sit dejected because you can find no more thought systems that can give you the answers you seek.

Perhaps the rejection of these various thought systems should be a clue to you about who you truly are, and where you should be looking for the answers to the universe. The answer does not lie outside of you but within you. Look inside and you will see all the miracles the cosmos has to offer. Look inside and you will see the past, present, future and more. Time is but a moving stream into and out of which you step on a daily basis. It may feel to some of you that you exist in only one dimension – in only one place – at a time, but this is false. All of us, whether we realize it or not, are multidimensional beings. We step in and out of different time periods all day, every day. You don't realize this fact and do not remember going to so many other places, times and dimensions because it would be overwhelming for your minds at their current state of development. However, many of you are beginning to have a sense of being in different times, places and dimensions. You are not fully aware yet but the beginning of sensing "something different" is happening. It might come in the form of strange dreams that look and feel so real, yet do not seem to quite correlate to your life as you know it. It might come in the form of a feeling of déjà vu or lightheadedness when you feel an energy pass through your aura.

Why is this happening and what is the point? This is happening because humanity is beginning to wake up to the true nature of reality. The true nature of reality is that all things, all time periods, all dimensions, coexist at the same time and in the same place. The universe is not something that is "out there". Rather, it is something that is in you right now. When you look at and see the planets and stars, or even your fellow human beings, you must understand fully that you are seeing yourself. You are in all things and beings, just as all things and beings are in you. There is no separation between the Earth's crust and you. There is no meaningful difference between you and the tree in your front yard. To many of you this will sound ludicrous. "I am not a tree!" many of you will wail. But we beg to differ. You are a tree, you are a rock, you are a cockroach, you are an angelic being, you are energy and you are light, among other things. You are all things wrapped up in a cute, little physical body at the moment. And one day you will still be all these things, just in another dimension and vibrating at a slightly different frequency.

What do you, a tree, a rock, and a bug all have in common? Life force – you are all energetic beings. You all vibrate at a slightly different frequency, but you all vibrate with an energy that never dissipates and can never be destroyed or eradicated. Energy is eternal and energy is life force, which means you are eternal beings – your essence, your life force, can never be destroyed or eradicated. No matter what you see going on around you in the next few years, you must remember that all life and all life force continues forever, just in slightly different circumstances and forms.

43

Live in the Present

THE JOY OF LIVING is being in the present and living life to the fullest, without concerns about what the future holds and what boons await. To live life to the fullest one must be in contact with one's inner being. Being in contact with one's inner being merely means being in contact with the basic life force that runs through each of us. In order to be in contact with the life force that runs through each of us, all we have to do is be aware of the present and what is occurring around us. Look around you now and see what is there. Is there a table, a lamp, a child, a pet? Whatever is around you is the present. Look around you and observe what is around you, if you want to be aware of the present. Don't let your mind wander to events of the day, or project into the future what you will do later or tomorrow. This is the key to understanding and living in the present. Periodically throughout the day look around you and see what is there. This is how to live in the present. This grounds you in the here and now. This grounds you in reality as it is. This is the key to understanding the future and what it will bring.

44

Forgive and Be Compassionate

THE TIME IS COMING when man will no longer need to look back in horror at what he has created. The time is coming when man will no longer look to the future with apprehension and fear of what will be. The time is coming when man will need only to look within his own heart to see what lies ahead. There is a time coming when all of humanity will rejoice at what has transpired and how it got there. There is a time not far on the horizon that will be filled with wondrous blessings and forgiveness of ourselves and others.

It is forgiveness of ourselves and others that will play a large role in ushering in this new state of being and existing. We have to let go of the grievances and hurts of yesterday if we are to bring in a new and more peaceful way of interacting with each other and the world at large. The world at large in this case means animals, plants and the planet itself. There are many people among you today who hold grudges against others and life itself. This grudge against life is causing and will continue to cause a great number of occurrences, which will disrupt everyday life and in some cases even extinguish some lives. This grudge against humanity and life itself is very destructive and goes back many generations. A grudge held only in this lifetime is powerful, but a grudge held for many lifetimes has an amplified destructive ability. This is the force which many today are dealing with and trying to come to terms with.

Many of you will be able to let go of the grudges you have been holding for lifetimes. However, many of you will not. Indeed, some of you will look around you and, seeing the events that are about to transpire, will actually strengthen your hatred of humanity and the gift of life. It is to these people that it is paramount to reach out. It is these people that can bring down humanity, or prevent humanity from moving forward as a group on the evolutionary path of enlightenment. Again we say it is to these people each of you must reach out and show kindness and mercy. Otherwise, you will be doing no more to help humanity on its evolutionary path than they are! It would be so easy if all we had to do was focus on ourselves and live in our own little world of our creation. This is not how life is. We are all connected, we are all one. Therefore, this person you see who hates life and hates everyone around her/him is also you. How he/she thinks and acts will influence how you think and act and vice versa. Work hard to show kindness and humility to this person. Work hard to show this person there are people who care about humanity, who are grateful for life and grateful this person is alive, and you will be helping humanity move forward on the path of enlightenment. Do nothing and you will wither and die on your path to so-called enlightenment. Enlightenment is about thinking and doing...not just pondering the meaning of existence or the theory of relativity. Actions speak louder than words and actions backed by a loving and compassionate intent have the most impact of all.

This is one reason compassion is so important. Compassion is backed by unconditional and true love. There is no power greater than true love, unconditional love. We are asking each of you reading this book to think about what act of compassion you have seen today or heard about today. How did it make you feel? Did it inspire in you a renewed faith in humanity, or did it make you want to tear up the furniture in your house? Of course it made you feel "warm and fuzzy". Seeing or hearing about that random act of kindness made you feel light and soft. It also kindled in your heart compassion for others and a willingness to help those less fortunate than yourself.

This is the point – those who by their actions or words demonstrate that they hate humanity or life should be held in the highest compassion. This is how the cycle of destruction and ruin will come to an end. This is how you will get from here to there – "here" being misery and suffering and "there" being joyfulness and bliss. Have compassionate thoughts about those in power and about those who wreak destruction on humanity, whether through folly, stupidity, greed or abuse of power. You do not need to condone their actions, but know in your heart these people are acting out of great pain and suffering. That is enough – just know they are acting out of great pain and suffering. Once you understand this – that their actions are based on their own great suffering, be it mental, psychological, physical, or spiritual – you will be able to feel compassion in your heart toward these individuals. Your feelings of compassion will help end the misery and suffering these individuals feel, and humanity feels as a group. This is how you, an individual, can do his/her part in helping humanity walk the tightrope of existence these next few years, and come out on the other side having advanced to a new stage of being.

The next few years will not be all bad for some of you, although most of you will at one time or another know pain and suffering. With the massive changes and upheavals likely to occur in the next few years it would be unwise to think you will not suffer at some point. However, suffering does not have to be extreme or taken to heart. By "taken to heart" we mean it does not have to stay with you and block your ascension to a higher state of being. The purpose of life is not, as many believe, to suffer hardship. We suffer hardship because we refuse to let go of the negative patterns of thinking and acting that then have a negative impact on our psyches and on our world. Remember, we create our own world. Our thoughts attract similar thoughts. Thoughts are energy and once a critical mass of energy is reached these thoughts manifest into "reality".

In the times ahead, remember to let go of negative thought patterns, like blaming others for our own "failings" when the fault always lies with you. No one is to blame because no one but you created your world. You are the ultimate creator and the ultimate destroyer. You can choose how we proceed. Do we have more death and destruction, or do we enter rapidly into an existence of unconditional love and peace? It is your choice. The actions you take will decide humanity's fate. We are quickly coming to the point of no return for many catastrophic events. Change your thoughts and feelings today, and we have a good chance of averting the major points of destruction that have been forecast for millennia. Have compassionate thoughts for those around you. Show compassion to a child or animal. Create more compassionate energy by forgiving those who have wronged you. Forgive those who cut you off in traffic or those who stab you in the back. Forgiveness and compassion are the only things that matter at this stage. Focus on these as if your life depended on it…because it does. Well, in a manner of speaking it does.

At this stage of human development your focus should be on spiritual pursuits and not money, power or success. Focus on your heart and cultivate feelings and thoughts of compassion and forgiveness, because that is all that matters. The only thing that is eternal is the spirit. The body is not eternal. Money is not eternal. Power is not eternal. Look inward and focus on your heart. Let compassion and forgiveness become your truth and see where it leads you. This truth will not lead you to death and destruction. This truth will lead you to eternity, to peace, to happiness and to unconditional love. In short, this truth will lead you to a new and elevated state of consciousness – to a new existence.

45

Activate New Energies

THE EVENTUAL EVOLUTION of humanity depends on the actions and thoughts occurring now. No thought, no action, is wasted at this time. We are in a time of heightened awareness and sensitivity to our surroundings. This means that whatever you think or do at this specific point in time has the potential to radiate out through the space/time continuum in a way never before possible, at least not in your written history. The alignment of Earth with the center of the Milky Way has allowed specific energies to flow into your atmosphere and consciousness. These energies are here to help humanity make the leap into the next level of consciousness.

While these energies are available to all on your planet, they must nonetheless be "activated". To activate these energies all you have to do is to pull these energies deep within your solar plexus and hold them there for a few minutes, then slowly release them back into the universe. This activation process need only be done once. Doing it more than once will not increase the amount or potency of these energies. These energies must be activated (or rather "reactivated") because it has been a very long time since man has been aware of and made use of these specific energies. Once these energies have been reactivated within your energy system and your consciousness, you will begin to see a difference in the world around you. You will find that that which used to bother you no longer bothers you. You will find that what used to make you angry no longer makes you angry. These energies you are reactivating are the energies of peace and unconditional love. These energies have not been present in your consciousness to this extent for a very long time. The time has now come for these energies to reassert themselves in your consciousness, so that humanity may, as a group, evolve to the next higher stage of being.

Not everyone will consciously choose to reactivate the energies of peace and unconditional love, also known as compassion. However, even those who do not consciously choose to reactivate these energies will receive benefit from those who do consciously choose the path of forgiveness and compassion. Your thoughts will influence the thoughts of those open to these energies, even if they are unaware of it. By your actions you will help lead others to the path of forgiveness and compassion.

There will be those among you who consciously shun the path of forgiveness and compassion, and for these individuals not much can be done except to view them with love and compassion rather than anger, hatred or contempt. As we have said many times, your role is not to judge others for what you believe to be their failings, faults or misguided behavior. Every action in the universe has its place. Nothing is random. Nothing is without reason. It is just sometimes, which is most of the time, you are unaware of what greater purpose might be served by a certain action. Just because you are unaware of the greater purpose does not mean one does not exist. What we are telling you is that as long as you focus on your heart, on your soul, and follow the path of forgiveness and compassion you will be acting in accordance with the highest and truest nature of the universe, and will be aiding humanity in its goal to achieve enlightenment this time around.

Humanity has already experienced many leaps on the evolutionary path of consciousness. However, to date none have been as spectacular a transition as the one you are about to experience. The levels to which humanity now has the opportunity to reach are unprecedented in your consciousness. This is what makes it all the more exciting and exhilarating. As you sit reading this book you have within your grasp the keys to the universe, the keys to opening the mind of all restrictions, whether self-imposed or imposed by society and culture. We ask only that you do a few meditations and then remain aware of your thoughts and actions, and you will be able to transform not only yourself but humanity! Every journey begins with a single step. Each transformation of consciousness begins with a single individual. You can make a difference to humanity. Your thoughts and your actions can change the world. You will not have to wait decades or centuries for this change to occur. This change can and will occur in the blink of an eye.

Humanity is on the brink of an explosion – an explosion of consciousness and ideas. Humanity is at the tipping point. There is no turning back now. There is no time to wait and see what happens. You must commit yourself to the path of forgiveness and compassion now. The sooner you do this, the easier your life and future will become. As we have said before, some events and occurrences have been written in stone. These cannot change or be averted.

However, there are still so many disasters and "unpleasant" events that can be averted and avoided, if you will but commit to the path of love and forgiveness.

Hold these thoughts in your head as often as possible. Focus on these thoughts before you go to sleep and as soon as you wake up, and we promise you will see a difference in yourself, your life and the lives of those around you. We cannot emphasize this point enough – focus on love and forgiveness if you want to see a different world, if you want to see a world based on peace and kindness. This kind of world is possible, but changes must be made now in human consciousness. The end is not near but the beginning is. Open your hearts and minds to love and forgiveness and see what happens. You have absolutely NOTHING to lose, so start today.

46

Step Up to the Challenge

THERE IS NO NEED TO WORRY about the future. The future will always be there, whether in its current form or in another form. The point is that the future will always be there so there is no need to worry about a time when there is no future. You will always be alive in one form, one dimension, or another, so there really is no need to fear death or separation from loved ones, because you are linked together via the Universal Consciousness. In fact, all of your minds are linked and are one in the Universal Consciousness. The sum of all human knowledge is a part of you and encoded in your DNA. This is how we often reach out to you and connect, and how some among you are able to reach out and come up with groundbreaking ideas and inventions. There is nothing new in the universe. Everything you see on your planet today has already been created and forgotten before. In fact, it is true that more knowledge and information has been lost than exists in your visible realm today.

There is a totality about the universe of which humans are woefully ignorant. It will not always be this way, but that is where we stand at the moment. These words may sound harsh but you must understand just how little of the Earth and the universe you understand today. It is our wish that you will all step up to the challenge of the coming times, and aid your fellow humans in the process of becoming more forgiving and loving toward each other. Compassion and forgiveness are the only traits that will get you through the upcoming trials and tribulations. If you do not work hard to accept kindness and compassion into your hearts now, you will have a very difficult time ahead, because you will not understand why certain events are taking place, and why certain people seem to be so filled with rage and hatred. If you can start to nurture the feelings of forgiveness and compassion in your hearts today, when the time comes you will be able to see what is truly going on and why certain people are acting the way they are. These emotions of kindness and compassion will help you make sense of a world that is seemingly out of control and standing on its ear.

Separate yourself now from the feelings of greed, control and manipulation of others. Fill your heart instead with love and compassion. You will be amazed at what trials and even diseases will pass you by in the times to come, if you will but fill your heart and mind with feelings of love and compassion rather than hatred and contempt. Judge not yourself or those around you for all have a role to play. Just because you do not understand another's role does not mean it is not valid or that it is worthy of criticism. This may be the hardest thing for most of you to grasp and hold on to in the days, weeks, months and years ahead. We know this.

When you feel yourself moving away from love and compassion and into the space of hatred and contempt, bring yourself back. Know that you are responsible for the ugliness you will see in the world. You are not exempt from responsibility. This is why it is foolhardy and senseless for you to criticize others in the coming times, for you are responsible for it. You helped create the anger and frustration that will soon spill out into the universe and change your planet forever. Your thoughts and actions in this lifetime and in others created what you are seeing today. You are not blameless. You are not guilt-free. Take responsibility today by filling your heart with love and compassion for yourself and all those around you.

Forgiveness is like a magic wand that creates peace and harmony. Forgiveness can bring comfort in times of stress. Forgiveness can bring joy to a heart burdened with sadness. Forgiveness can bring hope to those who feel there is no way forward. Forgiveness is a magic elixir of life.

47

You Are the Universe

THE MYSTERY OF THE UNIVERSE and the Universal Consciousness is not really that mysterious after all. The universe and the underlying Universal Consciousness are based on the principle of unconditional love and gratitude. As long as you try to live your life according to these principles, you will be in balance and harmony with the universe and you will find peace and joy in your heart. We get out of sync with the universe when we remove ourselves from the protection and comfort of unconditional love and gratitude. This is how we move into the idea and concept of separateness, and it is this feeling of separation and disconnection from the universe and all within it that has driven humanity to the extremes of actions and reactions it is now experiencing. This is what has driven man to the brink of destruction. This is also what has filled men's hearts with feelings of desolation, fear and hopelessness.

You feel you are all alone because you have cut your connection with your divine self – that part of you that helped to create the universe and all within it. In every cell of your body there are little bits and pieces of the universe. You are not separate from the universe – you are one and the same. This is one of the most important concepts to understand. The atoms and molecules that make up your body are the same atoms and molecules that make up the physical universe. Likewise, the energy that makes up your soul and essence is the same energy that makes up the Universal Consciousness. The force that breathed life into the universe is the same breath that is within you. You are no less magnificent a being than the most glorious star system or wondrous galaxy. You are just as precious and complex a wonder of nature and creation as anything you can see or imagine. Be aware of your magnificence and be grateful. Never take yourself or life for granted.

There are immense possibilities awaiting you if you will only let yourself be aware of them and embrace them. Embrace life and all its changes and permutations, and do it with an open heart and sense of peace and the heavens and all their wondrous mystery will be opened to you. There are no secrets in the universe, nor is there knowledge that is forbidden to humankind. Only those who would wish to control you for their own selfish purposes would wish to hide knowledge that is freely available to all who seek it. There is nothing you cannot do and nothing you are forbidden to know.

The universe and all that is within it is yours. It is your playground. What you choose to do with it is also your choice. How you choose to live your life is up to you. Yes, even the quality of your life is in your hands. There are no victims in this world. Just as there are truly no victims, there is also not one among you who is not responsible for what is going on today. As we have said many times already, take responsibility for your thoughts and actions if you want to live in a better world. The thoughts and actions humanity has taken up to this point are what are manifesting today. If you want to live in a different kind of world, one of peace and plenty for all, change the way you think and behave and do it today. Only you can put an end to this cycle of destruction and despair. Only you can bring about a new world of peace and enlightenment. Only you can create change. Only you can create.

Humans are capable of vast creations – they just don't realize it yet. Humans have no idea of how much they are capable. You have been living life as if you are the victims of creation instead of the originators of it. Take control of your life and your world by harnessing and exploring your creative abilities. Take responsibility for your life and for the lives of others by acknowledging you are the creators of all that is. Nothing is outside of your control. Accept it and embrace it. Take an active role in your life and create the kind of world you want, by embracing and focusing on love and gratitude. Accept these principles at your core and watch how your life will change for the better. Live your life with love and gratitude at the forefront of your mind, and you will automatically align yourself with the universe and the Universal Consciousness. As your frequency or vibratory rate changes, so too will your life. New possibilities will open up for you, as will new information and a new understanding.

48

You Control the Outcome

THE DARK DAYS of hatred and retribution have not yet finished on your planet. In the times to come there will be acts of vengeance and violence that will take the lives of many. Some of these acts will be obvious while others will be less so. However, do not despair. The days of darkness and greed have just about come to an end as far as many of you are concerned. Many of you will use the events that are about to take place to turn over a new leaf, so to speak. Many of you will look around at what is about to transpire and declare that you want nothing more to do with it, and that you are willing to change your minds and your attitudes. Many of you will see the only way forward is that of love and compassion. Many of you will open your hearts to those less fortunate. Many of you will see there is no future in hatred and greed. You will see the time for these emotions and behaviors is at an end. Many of you will see the way ahead is that of light and wellbeing.

There will be no suffering as long as you remember to keep love and compassion in your hearts. Do not turn a blind eye to what is going on around you. Rather, look fully at it and feel it in your hearts. Feel the pain and the suffering. But instead of getting angry and feeling helpless know that you are never helpless, you are never alone and you are never without compassion. The universe has an infinite supply of compassion and unconditional love. It is just that these emotions and ideas have not been prevalent on your planet for quite some time. Take the next step forward and reach out and claim these thoughts. Feel love and compassion in your hearts. Make an effort to see life as one of infinite grace and beauty in all things, and you will create a different environment.

The answer does not lie in the heavens nor does it lie at the bottom of the ocean. The answer lies in your hearts and depends on your actions and thoughts. Make the effort to see life through the eyes of compassion and love. We did not say see all of life completely through the eyes of compassion and love. We know this is impossible at this time but just make an effort – an effort is all that is required to move humanity one giant step closer to enlightenment. When you are confronted with a situation in which you begin to feel anger, step back, take a breath and remember love and compassion. By just remembering these concepts you will have gone a long way in diffusing your angry thoughts. This will in turn help reduce the amount of anger and violence in the world. As you do this time and time again, you will see that it becomes increasingly easier to dissolve your feelings of anger and hatred toward certain individuals and situations.

Know in your heart that there is a plan for humanity, and it does not have to involve massive amounts of suffering. You choose suffering by continuing to feel pity for yourselves and anger toward those people and situations you feel you cannot control. You can control all situations and all outcomes if you choose to. Control is not the same as manipulation. Manipulation involves doing something and getting someone else to do something so you are the winner in some way. Control, on the other hand, involves directing the outcome. You can control your life so you have a strong say in how it proceeds. The future of your world is in your hands. You control the outcome. What you choose to do this moment will make a difference. You are neither helpless nor a victim of circumstance. You are in control of everything that goes on in your life. You are in control of everything that goes on in the world – you just don't realize it yet.

The end is not near but the future is – a future that is bright and clear and completely within your control. Minimize the suffering and despair that will be coming in the days to come by preparing yourself now to view life and the people in it with compassion and fairness. Do not go too far to one side or other. Stay centered and stay balanced in your soul by meditating and seeking guidance from within. Follow your heart and your intuition in all matters. The time to follow only logic has passed. You are in control but this means you will have to take full responsibility and look at life differently. You cannot just sit back and continue on the same way. You must take a stand and train yourself to look at life through the eyes of compassion and love.

49

There Is Nothing
Unknown or Unknowable

THE HEAVENS ARE ABOUT TO OPEN UP and pour out a new energy on to the Earth. This energy will bring a new perspective on life and living. This energy will facilitate the transition from one cycle of existence to another. The old cycle of existence you are quite familiar with – greed, corruption, and distrust. If these characteristics seem to have become more prevalent throughout your lifetime you are correct. At the end of a cycle things speed up and intensify, and this is what has happened to Earth over the last 20 years or so. These characteristics were always there, but they were not so apparent in so many people at the same time. There have always been the few among you who exhibited these traits, but now there has been an explosion of greed, corruption, violence, division and the pure worship of self above all others.

The new cycle of existence will be one of peace and harmony with yourself and the world around you. There will be no divisions or separations among people or animals. By the way, this is why the killing of animals for sport and food will cease. Humans will no longer have dominion over the animals – this is how some of you view the world order. Humans will no longer see themselves as superior to the rest of creation. Humans will come to realize they are but one cog in the wheel of creation, in the wheel of the universe. Humans are neither more important nor less important than any other creature or being on this planet. Humans are no more important than a tree, really. You all serve a vital function – humans, trees, plants, animals, fish, seaweed, etc. – and without any one of you the ecosystem and the world could not continue to exist, and forget about flourishing! This is what it means to be at one with yourself and all that is around you. When you are at one, you realize you are neither more important nor less important than anyone or anything else. You see that balance and moderation are key to existence, and that when there is balance and moderation there is a harmony, from which a new world and new existence can be created and experienced.

Happiness is in your heart. Happiness comes from your heart. Nothing on the outside, nothing external, can bring true and lasting happiness. Happiness is a joy that springs from your openness to life. Your willingness to embrace life and the changes and challenges it brings will determine how much happiness you are capable of feeling. The more you are willing to embrace life, the more happiness you will feel. When we say "happiness" we are not talking about laughter and smiles only. We are also talking about being able to meet life's challenges head on without fear and regret. Happiness is also to be found in life's most difficult moments, such as the death of a loved one or the loss of an important job. Happiness comes about when we are able to see life for what it really is, when we are able to fully experience and embrace all the moments of life. Every moment of life is an expression of the divine. If you do not like the reference to divinity you can substitute the word "universal" and say every moment of life is an expression of the universal.

The universal is where all of life and creation originated and to where all of life and creation will return one day. What has come before is what will be in the future, and what will be in the future is what has come before. All of reality is in existence right now, waiting for your discovery and exploration. There is nothing that is unknown or unknowable, no problem that is unsolved or unsolvable. All that has ever been and all that will ever be already is, right here, right now. This is another key point to focus on and to remember – all that has ever been and all that will ever be already is, right here, right now. There is nothing new in the universe. Why is this important? Because once you accept that all that will ever be has already been, you will see the cyclical nature of the universe and begin to understand your place in it. You are a never-ending life and consciousness. This will never change.

You need not fear being alone or without food or without someone for an instant, because in the blink of an eye all that can change and will change if you but believe you are the creators of your own world and lives. Nothing is out of your control, nothing is impossible for you, nothing. All the information, all the guidance, all the reassurance, all the love you will ever need is out there. All you have to do is open your hearts to life and stop being afraid. Stop fearing the lack of something, be it money, charm, love, or kindness. Realize that anything you could possibly need has already been created and exists in the human consciousness. The point of telling you this is not so you will not exacerbate the current problems on Earth by becoming greedy and seeking more wealth to stoke your ego. The point in telling you this is so you will be able to let go of fear. Fear has held you back and prevented so many of you from moving forward or having truly happy lives. Remember, fear blocks positive energies. Fear holds you in a negative pattern of thinking, acting and behaving. When you release fear, you allow positive energies to flow in and when this happens your view of the world and life will change for the better.

50

Stay within Yourself

Y OU ARE NOT A CRACKPOT OR NEW AGE JUNKIE. You know the end is not near. You know in your heart the end is not near, but a new beginning for humanity is near, right around the corner. However, you also know that in order to get around that corner there will have to be some difficult times for you and for others. The time is coming when there will be very little water and food because these will have been polluted from one source or another. However, with the right thinking and right approach to these situations the suffering will be relatively short-lived, although not all will approach the situation as it should be approached. For these people the suffering will be long lasting. You will not be among these individuals. There will be a division among people soon – those who accept the new ways and the new way of being and those who do not.

Again we say – do not judge or condemn those who do not choose the new way of living. They do not do so because it is not in their highest interest to do so, just as it *is* in your highest interest to do so at this point in time. Do not concern yourself with others in terms of trying to "save" them or turn them to the light. You may mention what you are doing and invite them along, but if they show resistance let them be on their way. The universe is a complicated world in which we all have our part to play in order to achieve enlightenment. The people who do not choose to turn to the light and seek an end to the suffering are also playing their part – you just cannot see it right now but soon you will understand how all the parts fit together to create the whole. The whole is more than you could ever imagine and more beautiful than you could ever fathom.

There is a rhyme and a reason to everything that happens in the universe whether you see it or not. There is so much more going on than you could ever imagine. We tell you this so you will be better able to accept that there will be certain ways people will behave in the future that will make absolutely no sense to you. Do not try to make sense of their actions or words. Stay within yourself and seek the Universal Consciousness. Help to raise global consciousness and you will have done enough, more than enough really.

Soon people will start behaving in irrational and somewhat comical ways. There is nothing wrong with them per se other than their world as they know it, one based on a material hierarchical power structure, has started to collapse. In response to this they will be running like chickens with their heads cut off trying to make sense of their reality. Do not worry – none of these people will bring you any harm. Observe them, wish them enlightenment and move on. Do not get caught up in the day-to-day traumas that will begin to unfold shortly. Stay centered and in the observer mode, knowing the only thing that really matters at this time is what you are doing for your soul and to advance the cause of humanity toward a more enlightened way of being.

51

Weigh Your Decisions

EVERYTHING IS NOT ALWAYS WHAT IT SEEMS. Just as every action is not always what it seems, there are some actions in this world that are taken to protect and illuminate humanity. There are other actions in this world that are self-serving and manipulative. The key in the upcoming times will be to know what actions are in your highest interests and which are not. There will be many actions taken fast and furiously in the coming days, and you will need to be able to ascertain which decisions are for your greatest good and which are not. The last thing any of you want to do now is complicate your life or your path.

Complications will arise by the very nature of life itself. You cannot anticipate all events and incidents. However, you can prepare yourself to be able to make the swiftest and best choice. You can do this by starting to ground yourself now. Whenever you have a decision to make, just sit back for a moment. In this moment think and feel the weight of this decision. Feel the heaviness of it and then ask your higher self which decision feels right. For the "wrong" decision you will feel a heaviness in your body. For the "right" decision you will feel a lightness in your solar plexus. This goes for all of you. No one will have the polarities reversed for this test of which is the "right" or "wrong" decision. The polarities are universal for this one.

Start weighing your decisions today so when the crunch time comes you will be able to fly on your feet with decisions. This is important because life will begin to speed up. If some of you are sitting thinking to yourself that life has already sped up, you are right. Now, magnify that increase in speed by a factor of about 20 and you will have an idea of how fast life can get. Not all of you will experience life approaching so quickly. Some of you will be able to successfully slow life and the events in your life down to a more manageable level. However, many of you will not focus on grounding and on your core, and thus will not be able to slow down your universe or your experience of it. To slow down your universe is not difficult. With a little practice all of you can do it almost without effort. The key to manipulating matter and energy is not so difficult once you understand the basic principles. One of those "basic principles" is grounding and reaching in to your core, because your core is the universe! By reaching within you are touching the universe. The universe is found within you as well as outside of you, but it is that which is within you that has the most power to create and destroy. Whatever feat can be accomplished in the external universe, that which you see around you can be done 200 times faster and more effectively by utilizing the internal universe.

No one will be able to stop the person or people who have truly connected to their internal universes. Of course this power to create and destroy is neutral, so it can be used for the betterment of humanity or for its destruction. This is one of the wars that will be raging in the coming years – that between those who want to help humanity evolve, and those who want to destroy humanity for their own gain. More people are needed who have reached in, touched their core and are willing to use this power for the betterment of man. While the war is almost won, there are still many battles awaiting humanity and many decisions to make on a personal and societal level. Each of these decisions will lay the cornerstone of the future.

Again, the future is by no means written in stone. There is a general framework that has been decided by humanity, but the final details have not yet been decided. This is why it is so important for each of you reading this book to reach inside and do what you can to help humanity evolve to the next level. You are not here to convert people to your way of thinking. You are here to help steer humanity in the direction of enlightenment by forming enlightened views and taking enlightened actions. If someone comes to you for guidance, help them to the best of your ability, but do not go out of your way to find strays and try to bring them back into the fold. We have already told you several times that everyone has a role to play in the upcoming events, and you must follow your path but not judge those who for reasons unclear to you decide to follow another. Their decisions are none of your concern. Focus first on cleaning your house before you start working to clean another's. You cannot control the thoughts or actions of others but you can control and direct your own. So keep this in mind when people start acting strangely. Keep yourself focused and healthy, and all will fall into place quite naturally and quickly.

52

Never Forget
Who and What You Are

HUMANITY IS ABOUT TO TURN A CORNER – a corner that will lead it to destruction or to bliss. Destruction comes in many forms and is not just physical. There can be destruction of the soul, destruction of the spirit, destruction of hope, destruction of sanity. Destruction of the soul – not the eternal one but the one you consider to be your life force while in your current body, the essence of who you are in this lifetime – is perhaps the most devastating destruction possible. It is the destruction of this part of you, of who you think you are in this lifetime, that you must work hard to avoid. There will be people and forces who will shortly begin to appear and gain power that will attempt to destroy man's belief in who he is and what he is. Do not let these beings and forces remove you from your core belief of who and what you are. You are a being capable of tremendous power and full of unconditional love. There will be people and forces soon who will attempt to divide humanity – they will attempt to turn neighbor against neighbor. Always remember who and what you are – a being of light and love, capable of tremendous joy and compassion. You are not a dark and evil creature who has led humankind to its destruction. You are not an awful creature who is self-serving and self-centered. You are a creature of compassion and intelligence who has forgotten how to use these qualities to help humankind in one of its darkest hours of need.

Go within yourself and seek out these qualities of compassion and goodness. Nurture these qualities and see how they grow and expand. Be kind to the people in your life and the people you meet on the street. Be kind to the person who curses at you. Know that your actions now, how you react to everyday situations, will make a difference to the state of human consciousness. This difference will not take months or years to filter into the global consciousness, but will do so immediately and with great positive effect.

Look within your heart and forgive those who have wronged you, forgive yourself for having wronged yourself, and forgive those who have come before you and left the world in the state it is currently in. When you have done this, move on to the next higher level of existence by loving all creatures. Love the ant that bites you at your picnic; love the bird that messes up your just-washed car; love the dog that barks all night for no apparent reason. Show love to all who cross your path by showing them kindness and forgiveness. If you get angry at someone, immediately stop and see what you are doing. Forgive yourself for getting angry and then forgive that person for pushing your buttons.

Know that the quicker you are to show forgiveness, the greater the positive effect will be in the Universal Consciousness. As you forgive yourself, others will begin to forgive you, for you are no perfect, little angel pure as the driven snow. No, you have flaws and faults just like everyone else – this is why you must first forgive yourself and then others. As more and more forgiveness is generated, more and more goodwill will be created among humanity, and as this happens tension and hatred levels will begin to dissipate. As these levels begin to dissipate there will be a spontaneous rising of the Universal Consciousness, and as this happens it will become increasingly easier to exhibit kindness and forgiveness to all living creatures. As each step builds upon the previous step, humanity will begin to move en masse into a new realm of existence – one that is peaceful, loving and harmonious. Humanity will begin to see the world around them with different eyes. The blinders that have held man back for eons will finally be removed and man will see and experience reality as it really is.

This is what is in store for humanity.

53

Responsibility to Yourself
and Humankind

FORGIVENESS IS NOT THE SAME AS COMPASSION. Compassion is about opening your heart and letting in the unity of a feeling or an emotion. Forgiveness is about opening your heart and letting in trust and letting go of fear.

Fear is your only enemy in this world. All other so-called enemies – persecution, starvation, death, and crime – can be mitigated or avoided altogether if only you will remove fear from the equation. Fear amplifies negative emotions and actions. An action that is done out of fear will have serious repercussions for all concerned – and even those not directly involved – because the fear and the result of the action it inspired will be dispersed throughout the Universal Consciousness. The Universal Consciousness is neutral, which means it cannot filter out negative emotions, thoughts or actions. As you put into the Universal Consciousness, so will you create. If you put in fear and hatred, this is what you will create and manifest for your world and reality.

The Universal Consciousness is a collective consciousness, which means each of you are responsible for what you put in, and what you put in affects everyone else in the world, just as what others put in affects you. One cannot negate or stop the flow of the Universal Consciousness. What has been put in must play itself out. However, what you can do and what you must do at this time is stop putting in more feelings, thoughts and actions based on hatred and fear. The amount of hatred and fear already in the Universal Consciousness must play out – it must manifest itself into concrete reality as you know it, and when it does you will be shocked by its ferocity. You will begin to see just how destructive hatred, anger and fear are.

There is a lag time between when a thought or result of an action enters the collective consciousness and when it manifests as physical reality. When a thought enters the collective consciousness, which is immediately upon the thought being thought – actually, slightly before but we don't need to be that exact for this point, it kind of "floats" around as more and more similar thoughts attach themselves together. When this thought has gathered enough similar thoughts (remember, thoughts are energy and like attracts like), when it has reached "critical mass", then and only then is it manifested into the physical – your reality as you currently know it.

Now, as you might have guessed, a whole lot of fear, hatred and anger has been released into the collective consciousness over the last hundred years, especially over the last 20 or so. The more people on the planet, the more thoughts there are. The more similar thoughts there are, the greater the destructive ability of that single type of thought. If you have two billion people having thoughts of anger and violence, when those thoughts meet up in the collective consciousness they will create a more devastating event in the physical reality than if you only had half a billion people having thoughts of anger and violence.

Likewise, if you have two billion people thinking thoughts of love and forgiveness, there will be a much greater positive event for humanity than if you only had 100,000 people having these thoughts.

By consciously controlling and focusing your thoughts, you can make a difference in the world and help humanity enter a Golden Age of existence. You can bring peace and harmony to the world. You can end bloodshed and violence. You can end poverty and famine. You can do all these things and more if you will just be conscious of your thoughts, pay attention to what you are thinking and when you see a thought of fear, hatred, violence, anger, repression, oppression, control, manipulation, jealousy, vengeance, or greed, be aware of it and forgive yourself and then forgive the person or situation that gave rise to the negative thought in you.

It is not too late to mitigate the physical effects of some of the thoughts of fear and hatred that have been released into the collective consciousness; however, it is too late to mitigate all of them. This is just a fact and just as certain is the fact that as a result certain devastating events will unfold in the not-too-distant future. However, this devastation and destruction does not have to continue or grow in intensity. It is certainly not too late to create a new reality – one of peace and harmony – and this can be done by watching and being aware of your thoughts. Change how you react to other people and the events going on around you. Anchor yourself in love, kindness, compassion ad forgiveness and you will be able to create this new environment. You will see a difference first in your own life and then you will be able to see the positive effect your thoughts and actions have on society.

It sounds simple, doesn't it? In a way it is so simple. However, it is also extremely difficult because in order to change the world, to bring peace upon Earth, to end hunger and poverty, to end cruelty and punishment, you are being asked to let go of the emotions you seem to hold most dear – fear, anger and hatred. You are being asked to be aware of yourself and your thoughts and to acknowledge responsibility for your thoughts and actions. No more can you blame someone else. No more can you say if only "those people" had not moved into my neighborhood, town, city, country, we would not have these problems. You created the anger, hatred, violence, mistrust, and destruction. You created the chaos you see around you. You are responsible for the pain and suffering in your life and in this world. You created it yourself and you alone are responsible.

Now, forgive yourself. Release your guilt, fear, blame, self-consciousness, judgment and conceit – release all these cancerous, negative and destructive emotions and replace them with thoughts of love, kindness, hope, and compassion. You can do this. You can replace your negative emotions and thoughts with positive ones, but only if you remain aware of your thoughts and emotions. Do not become lazy again. Do not shirk your responsibility to yourself and to humankind. Admit you are the creator of your world and everything in it. Embrace this fact – do not be frightened by it. Welcome your own creative power back into your life and the world. Create the reality you came here to create – one of peace and harmony. This will be a true testament to the power and glory of the human potential.

Do not give up now. The race is almost won. The time of darkness and despair is almost over. Just hang on a little longer, open your heart, mind and ears to love, compassion, and forgiveness, and the war will be over. No more will you witness cruelty, violence and destruction. No more will your heart bleed at the suffering and misery all around you because there will be no more misery and suffering. There will only be happiness and bliss, joy and contentment. These are attainable in this lifetime on this planet and at this time – all you have to do is be aware of your thoughts.

54

Let Go of Fear

FEAR IS THE MOST DESTRUCTIVE FORCE ON THIS PLANET. Because of fear, people do, say, and think things they would never otherwise do, say or feel. Fear is at the root of all discord, unhappiness and conflict within oneself and within society. Fear is the only "sin" because without fear there would be no gang rape, no killing, no starvation and no suffering. Fear is what brings all these terrible things upon humanity. We have allowed fear to creep into our minds, hearts and souls and now we witness fear and fear-mongering on a grand and staggering scale. Fear has evolved to the point where a day does not pass that you do not feel a bolt of fear – whether it is fear that you will lose your job, fear that you will lose your life savings, fear that your child will be hit by a car or abducted, fear that you will not live up to your image of yourself – which of course is a false image based on ego, fear that you will not be able to find a parking space at the mall, or any other fear you care to imagine. The point is we are bundles of fear, ready to snap at any time.

Do not allow fear to control your life any longer. Let go of fear and as you do life will get remarkably easier and less complex. You will no longer have to second-guess what your boss meant by "that comment" because without the drain of fear on your psyche you will know automatically what your boss meant by "that comment". You will be able to see comments for what they are. If someone makes a statement that is false, you will automatically be able to sense that it is a lie. You will not doubt yourself, you will not use precious energy running in circles wondering if the statement is true or not – you will know automatically and be able to take the appropriate action.

This brings us to the issue of discernment. In the near future, indeed now, it is paramount to be able to discern when people are telling the truth. You need to be able to sift through the chatter and see the bigger picture – to know what is really going on behind the scenes and what lies behind their words. There will be many people who will try to mislead you. Some of these people will do it honestly, which means they have no "evil" intent behind what they are doing because they honestly believe it is for your own good. However, there are many more who are motivated by an agenda – an agenda that is not in your highest good. These are the people and times we are warning you against. It is for these times that you must learn to center yourself and discern what is really being said and what is really going on. If ever you are in doubt, you can use this "decision method" – simply ask yourself if what this person is saying is true. If you feel a weight in the pit of your stomach, in your solar plexus, it is not true. If, on the other hand, you feel an energy coursing upward through your body, you can be sure it is indeed true. We give you this fallback test, the "decision method" discussed earlier in this book, because many of the lies you will be told will be so bold you will say to yourself that surely this must be the truth – they would not lie so openly about something like this. Well, they will and many of the people will be very skillful at gaining your trust.

Connect with your inner core, your inner being. Trust in yourself and in your direct connection with the divine. Do what feels right to you. Don't follow the masses because that is what everyone else is doing. Follow you own heart and your own instinct, and you will not be lead astray nor will you suffer any unnecessary hardships. In fact, if you follow your heart (a heart not filled with fear and contempt) you will be much happier while you are waiting to cross over into the next higher level of consciousness. Everyone will cross at the time that is right for them. Some people already have crossed while others are fully aware of the date and time of their crossing (not death). Still others are pretty much clueless as to when or if they will jump to the next level of consciousness. It doesn't matter because those of you who have decided to exist on this higher plane of consciousness in this lifetime will do so when the time is right.

Divine guidance will never lie to you nor will it lead you astray or off your path. The problem is we as humans are not always that good at hearing divine guidance clearly. Often we interject our own beliefs or ideas onto whatever the divine guidance is saying, and in a way we "hijack" the message to suit our own purposes and agendas. We do this because we need to control our lives. We need to feel in control of our futures. In reality, what we should be doing is listening with an open mind and open heart to divine guidance. Being "in control' and "creating" are not the same thing. When we seek to control something we do so out of fear – fear of getting hurt, fear of losing something or someone, fear that someone or something will get the better of us.

If you truly believe you have the ability to create the events in your life, you have no reason to be afraid because all the power is in your hands. This power is only non-destructive when you have awakened spiritually, when you let go of the fears and negative emotions that consume so many of us. If you harness this creative power before you have awakened your spiritual side sufficiently, you will create a lot of destruction and heartbreak in your life. You will know when you have awakened spiritually when you see you have no need for material possessions, when you feel no jealousy or anger toward your neighbor, when you can see clearly that all humans are filled with unconditional love and compassion. When this has happened you will be deemed responsible enough to wield the keys of the universe and have all its mysteries put in your hands. Until then, continue to work on yourself spiritually by focusing on kindness, forgiveness and compassion. Do not let others lead you away from yourself and your personal connection with the divine. Know that this is the most important thing you can do to prepare for the times ahead. There is nothing more important at this time.

55

Your Greatest Gift
to Humankind

THE YOKE OF RESPONSIBILITY is on us all. We must all do what we
can to help make the transition to the next stage of conscious evolution as easy
as possible, and to include as many people as possible. For some this will seem
like a heavy burden while for others it will be as light as a feather. We are all at
different stages of our personal and spiritual development. There is not a large
group leading the way because they are so much more developed spiritually
than the rest of us. This is why you should not be looking to the outside for
someone to show you the way or to lead you out of destruction's way. We have
all developed different parts of us at different rates. Some of us have focused on
the material aspect of our lives more than our spiritual development. Others
have focused on certain characteristics such as serving humanity, or protecting
endangered species from extinction. Still others have focused on scientific
pursuits or improving machines. Whatever has been the focus of your life and
your life's work, it is now time to redirect your energies toward that which will
have a lasting influence on humanity – your soul's development.

By focusing on your soul at this time in history, you will be
contributing to the evolution and elevation of human consciousness on Earth.
This is the greatest gift you could give humankind. This is the greatest hope
you could give humankind. This, above all else, is why you are here on Earth
at this time. This is the time you have been waiting for. This is why you have
been through cycle after cycle of existence. This is what you have all been
waiting for – the moment when you were standing on the edge of conscious
evolution, the moment when you would remember who you are and what you
are capable of being and doing. You have been waiting for the moment when

the universe and all the laws within it would make sense to you once again. When there would be harmony and peace in your soul regardless of what was going on around you. This is the moment you have been awaiting for eons – the moment when you would be reconnected with yourself and your inner core, and by so doing be reconnected with the majesty of the universe and all its creations. This is your ultimate goal. This is your dream. This is what you have been waiting for.

The end is not near but the beginning is – the beginning of a new existence on Earth. The veil that has shielded your eyes from your true self will now be lifted and you will see with perfect clarity who and what you are. You will begin to see with great clarity where you came from and where you are going. For the last eon it has been as if humanity was just walking in circles – one step forward, one step backward – but never really getting anywhere in particular. This is about to change.

Soon you will see massive forward progression. It has been a long time since true spiritual progression was seen on this planet. This is what you have been waiting for. This is what you have been preparing for. This is the moment when all will change in the blink of an eye. This is the time when your neighbor will seemingly transform overnight into an enlightened spiritual being. This is the time when men who once cursed each other and thought only of ways to kill each other will seemingly overnight be able to put their differences aside and embrace one another with love, compassion and true forgiveness on a soul level.

These are the times in which you are now living; all these things are possible and more if you will but just focus on your inner core and nurture your soul. Nurture your soul by focusing on forgiveness, unconditional love, kindness and compassion. This is the world you want to create, so focus on these things and it will soon become a reality. This is how the principles of creation work – directed thought or focus brings about a physical reality or physical manifestations. You are neither a victim nor a pawn. You are a creator of life and reality. If you want more unconditional love, give more unconditional love. If you want more kindness and gentleness, be kinder and gentler with those around you. What you sow, so do you reap. Do unto others as you would have them do unto you. Think of others as you would have them think of you. One person can make a difference.

IV. There Are No Secrets

56

The Way Is Clear

THE WAY FORWARD is clear for all who care to see it. There is no mystery, nothing secret and nothing hidden about the way forward. The way ahead is marked with signposts for all to read. The universe is not playing a cruel trick on you. The universe is not out to get you. The universe is here to help if you will but reach out and understand what it is telling you. The way forward is clear. The way forward is predicated upon you reaching inside and re-establishing your connection with your inner core and with the universe yourself. You cannot wait for someone else to do it for you – only you can re-establish your connection with the universe, and that means you have to make the necessary changes in your life. No one can do it for you. Don't be misled by those around you who will tell you they have found an easy way to reconnect with the universe and to harness its creative abilities. Many of these people wish you harm.

There are forces on this planet that do not want to see humanity jump forward on the scale of evolution and live in harmony and peace. There are some among you who wish to see the destruction of humanity. There is a basis for the stories of the battles between light and dark that have been told for eons. There is such a force among you and it is the force of "evil". However, this force is not more powerful than that of love and compassion. There is a duality in the world today and this is what humankind is struggling with on a very fundamental level. This is the struggle that consciousness is going through. As humanity progresses to the next stage of development, to the next stage of existence, this lower form of consciousness will cease to exist. Consciousness is an energy and as such has a will to exist. This is the battle – the battle between a lower form of consciousness and a higher form – that will play out in the next few years. There are those among you who would have this lower form of consciousness continue, and these people will do all they can to see to it that this is what happens. However, this is not what will happen – not for those of you who choose to relinquish this lower form of consciousness and step onto a higher plane of existence.

The way ahead is clear for those who wish to see it. There are no real mysteries in the universe – all is an open book for those who care to see it. However, in order to "see it" clearly you must take responsibility and do the work that is required. The work that is required is for you to remain within yourself and show genuine love and compassion to those around you. Love and compassion are the seeds of light that will shine into the world and into eternity. Love and compassion are the cornerstones of the universe and all that is within it. It is love and compassion that will illuminate the world around you. It is through eyes filled with love and compassion that you will be able to see what is really going on around you. It is through eyes filled with love and compassion that you will be able to see what has been until now shrouded in mystery and behind the veil.

Only when you have filled your heart, mind and eyes with love and compassion will the "keys" to the universe be granted to you. These keys are not hidden and never have been, however, they will not be "apparent" until you open yourself to love and compassion. This is what is required for you to be able to change matter and space and to travel through time.

It may sound simple but removing the blinders by filling your heart with love and compassion will not be that easy. However, humankind is being given a tremendous opportunity to advance itself. Look around you and see in the despair the chance to show true compassion and true forgiveness. Today and in the next few years you will have more chances to show love and true forgiveness than you ever thought possible. You will squander most of these chances to show compassion and forgiveness. But that's okay because you only have to touch true compassion and forgiveness once to start your soul on the path of enlightenment. Once you have touched pure compassion and pure forgiveness these energies will begin building in your body, mind and spirit and will lead you to a course of action, to a way of thinking and to a way of being that will help humanity in its quest to achieve enlightenment and move forward on the evolutionary scale of development. Right now you are planting a seed that will grow and move humanity forward in incalculably wonderful directions. There is a new form of existence and a new reality waiting for you that cannot be described in terms of the words in your consciousness at this moment. There are feelings of exhilaration and contentment you have never felt before so there is no way you could have come up with a description – not yet at least. But you will.

Once the doors of this new existence have been flung open, you will never again want to come back into this existence. You will look upon this existence as something that was good while it lasted but now you have outgrown this mode of being, and are ready to move on to new challenges and a new way of perceiving reality. This is what is in store for humanity and this day is just around the corner, and is open to all who seek and make the effort. No one will be left behind – some of us will just start this new existence before others. We are all working according to our own timetable and that is why you should focus on yourself and your spiritual development and not worry about others. Help people if they come to you but do not seek them out. If you seek them out they might have the impression that you offer them some magic key that will help them jump the queue, so to speak, but no one can offer such a thing. Each individual must do the work required. There is no magic wand and there is no shortcut.

Having said this, there also is not just one path to enlightenment and the next stage of existence. This is another reason why it would be wrong of you to try to teach people your way. Answer people's questions but make sure they know your answers are for you only because they are "your way" to enlightenment. Some people's way may be the same as yours, or a combination of yours and someone else's, or have nothing whatsoever to do with yours! This is why you only offer information; what people choose to do with it is their own decision.

57

As Your Thoughts Go,
so Goes Humanity

THERE ARE BEAUTIFUL DAYS awaiting humanity. There are days of joy and peace awaiting humanity. These days can be here now for those who are able to move out of the existence they are currently in. You are not trapped in your current existence. You are free to move about the cabin, so to speak. You can move into other dimensions of existence right now if you choose to. In order to accomplish this, you have to first let go of the old paradigms holding you in place. You do this by expanding your consciousness through meditation, prayer and directed and highly focused thoughts. Do not let your thoughts randomly wander all over the place, touching on greed, anger, jealousy, hatred, fear, and annoyance. Focus your thoughts and limit them to the kind of world you want to live in. If you want to live in a peaceful world, have more thoughts of peace and harmony. If you want to live in a giving and caring society, focus your thoughts on these aspects. Direct your thoughts in such a way that they will not only help you but will also help humanity ascend to higher levels.

The time for humankind to take responsibility for its world has come; this means humankind can no longer plead ignorance of the laws of creation. As your thoughts go, so goes humanity. Each of your thoughts has relevance because each of your thoughts is energy. Many of your great spiritual masters have told you this and now your own science is telling you this. The time has come for humanity to take its share of responsibility and direct its future in a positive manner. This is why the end is not near but the beginning is. You are standing at a point in history when you have the chance to consciously direct the course of events. You can sit in the bubble in which you all have been living for eons, a bubble in which you felt powerless and disconnected from the universe, or you can take action now and step into the realm of peace and harmony, and restore your full creative potential by reconnecting with the universe and the Universal Consciousness.

Your future awaits you. You are responsible for your future. What you choose to do today will determine the course of your future. This is not to say there will be only peace and harmony in the future, because this is not the case. However, how you react to the upcoming events that have already been set in motion by past thoughts and actions is up to you and fully within your control. You can choose to be the powerless victim, or you can take responsibility by changing your thought patterns. Change your thoughts to those of joyful matters – peace, love, balance, forgiveness and harmony – and you will be creating a different future for yourself and others. Let go of what society has taught you about right and wrong. Let go of what your parents taught you about right and wrong. If you are truly connected with the universe and the Universal Consciousness you will know what is right and what is "wrong". By "right" we mean what will help humanity progress and by "wrong" we mean what will hold humanity in its current lower state of consciousness.

There is nothing "wrong" with the state of consciousness most of you are now in. It is just that at this moment you are being given a golden opportunity to progress forward on the evolutionary scale. Most of you have "outgrown" your current state of consciousness and this is why so many of you are looking to fill the spiritual void you now feel. The old religions no longer answer your questions or make sense. These religions and their teachings have become corrupt and seem to lead you astray from the fundamental principles of the universe, which are unconditional love, forgiveness, kindness, and tolerance. Few religions and few "religious" people are tolerant of those with whom they do not agree. Few "religious" people practice forgiveness and unconditional love. Few religions teach you how to go within yourself to seek answers. Few religions teach you of your own creative ability and your own power as a living, breathing part of the divine.

You have been disconnected from your divine element by people who wish to lead you astray and to remain dominant over you. The time has come for humankind to stand up and take back their divine element. You can reconnect with the universe and the Universal Consciousness to create a new reality and to step forward into a higher state of being and existence. The power is yours and the time is now.

58

The Calm of
Embracing New Paradigms

THE WORLD IS ABOUT TO CHANGE and the old way of thinking will come to an abrupt halt for many of you. Many of you, however, will continue along your old track of thinking and behaving. For you, the changes coming to this planet will be painful and heart wrenching. You will experience suffering to a degree you never thought possible. You will pray for death to take you but it will not – not until your time has come, and for some of you this is many years hence. For those of you who choose to continue thinking and behaving along the old lines, the old paradigm, here are a few of the events you have to look forward to: rashes and skin irritations which no ointment or cream will alleviate, solar flares which will cause blindness and sores on the skin, water contaminated by dead bodies and chemicals, air filled with the stench of unburied human remains, a planet littered with debris from satellites and space stations that will soon come crashing to Earth, volcanic ash in the atmosphere choking out the sunlight, mountains of debris as garbage and refuse piles up in city streets, because cities will no longer be able to afford trash collection. Life will become very difficult for a great many of you over the next few years.

However, for many of you life will just now start getting good! For many of you will have turned away from the old way of thinking and behaving, and will have started embracing a new paradigm of existence – a paradigm in which kindness, forgiveness and love are at the core. For those of you who have stepped into this new existence, the world will be a very different experience than for the rest of humanity. You will still experience heartache when you look around you and see the level of suffering and deprivation man is allowing to exist. However, you will be removed from the pain and torture of the soul that the rest of humanity will be experiencing, because your soul will have already aligned with the Universal Consciousness and its frequency. Your metaphoric heart – your ability to feel love and compassion – will have opened and will shield you from the worst of what is to come. You will witness the events but you will not be a part of the events or trapped in the events.

A calm will begin to settle over those who have turned to the new way of experiencing life. For those of you who have returned to your core, your essence, a new tranquility will guide your thoughts and actions. You will become more thoughtful about what you are doing and why you are here at this moment. You will understand why you are here and what your role is in helping humanity cross over to the next level of consciousness. Some of you will work directly with people while others of you will work indirectly, but all of you will be assisting humanity. Actions will no longer be self-serving – they will be serving humanity.

59

The Choice Is Yours

THE SPIRITUAL BEGINNING is just around the corner for many of you. In this spiritual beginning, or reawakening, there will be decisions to be made and actions to be taken. You will have laid before you a course of events that will require thought and action on your part. There are no right or wrong actions, only "wrong" thoughts. Thoughts of greed, anger, violence, mistrust, fear and competition are the "wrong" thoughts for you to have if your intent is to move into an awakened state of consciousness. If you want to stay in your current state of consciousness, these would not be the "wrong" thoughts to have. These would then become the "right" thoughts to have. The choice is yours and yours alone. There will be no person or group of people who will make the decision for you – only you can decide which road you want to travel and which existence you want to experience.

While there are many roads from which to choose, there are really only two outcomes possible at this time. One outcome is you stay at your current level of consciousness. The other is where you enter a new and different state of consciousness (new and different for you, that is). In the new state of consciousness you will once again be the powerful, magnificent creatures you truly are. You will tap into your inner core of strength, abundance, knowledge and wisdom, and will see and experience life and living from a different perspective – one of hope and love.

At this point, there are many things that could be said about what is likely to happen to those who wish to remain at their current level of consciousness. However, this book is not about fear-mongering or scaring people onto a certain path. The purpose of this book is to help people who want to shift their consciousness to do so in an easy and smooth manner. It is not complicated and it is not a long, drawn-out process. The method is transparent and straightforward – open your heart, follow your heart and return to a state of compassion and forgiveness. You do this by becoming aware of your thoughts and realizing there are no random thoughts – all thoughts are energy and, as energy, have the power to create or destroy. So choose your thoughts carefully and make sure they are consistent with what you want your life to represent. If you want your life to represent greed and intolerance, hold onto these thoughts. If you want your life to represent kindness and forgiveness, hold onto and nurture these thoughts. Every thought you have about someone else affects not only that person in a positive or negative way, but because we are all one it also affects you in the same way. There are no neutral thoughts – all thoughts carry a charge and have an effect.

60

Break through the Veil

THE FUTURE IS COMING whether you want it to or not. Changes are coming whether you want them to or not. You cannot stave off change just because you are fearful of it. There is no reason to fear change. Change brings with it an opportunity for accomplishment and success. Change brings variety and freedom from boredom.

The future is now. The changes that are soon coming to your world are changes you have created so you could have the opportunity to step into a new reality and a new phase of existence. Without these changes you would be stuck in your old mentality, your old way of behaving and your old way of responding to the world. With the changes that are coming, you will be able to more easily transcend your old mentality, way of behaving and way of responding to the world. The changes that are coming bring you a golden opportunity to open your eyes and your heart to see for the first time the world around you as it really is and was really meant to be. You, and the rest of humanity, have been trapped in a kind of time warp – a time warp in which your thoughts and actions fed back upon themselves in what seemed like an endless reverberation. This is the veil humanity is about to finally have the opportunity to break through.

You will no longer be trapped in this endless feedback loop in which you keep experiencing the same things but with more intensity each time. You will now be able to go out and create an entirely new world in which there will be new experiences, and instead of creating the same thing or event over and over again, each creation will be a totally new experience. Your world will be one of constant evolution and renewal, rather than cycle upon cycle of devastation and destruction. In the new existence, you have an opportunity to create a world without calamity and without chaos.

The choice is yours. Do you want to continue in this endless feedback loop of cycles, or do you want to step into a new and different reality in which people's thoughts and actions are based on mutual understanding, trust, unconditional love and forgiveness? For many of you the decision will be quite easy, while for others it will not. Do not judge others for the decision they make. Your role is not to decide what is best for others, but only what is best for you. In a state of compassion, there is no room for judgment or criticism. You can offer a helping hand but if it is refused do not be angry or sad, because we must each make our own decision about life and our chosen path. No one else can make the decision for you, just as no one else can take the responsibility for what results from our own thoughts and actions. We alone are responsible for the results of our thoughts and actions. There is no one else to scold or blame but us.

However, as soon as we realize we are responsible for what goes on in our private lives and in the rest of the world, we will drop the need to find excuses or blame other people. In time we will also understand that to blame ourselves is senseless. Because we create and control what happens in our world, there is no need to blame or criticize. If there is something in your world you do not like, change the thought that created it in the first place. If you are tired of living with fear, greed, destruction and hatred, change the thoughts in you that give rise to these actions in your world. Change your heart and you will change your world.

The end is not over but it soon will be. The "end times" will not last forever even though for some of you it will seem like an eternity. This is a time not to fear change but to embrace it because it is these changes that are giving you an opportunity to break with the past and the old paradigms and to create a new one in which you will find peace, harmony, love and compassion. Without the events that are about to occur this level of change would not be possible. This is what you have been waiting for all these lifetimes.

61

Your Greatest Transformation
Can Be Effortless

THERE ARE EVENTS about to happen on Earth that are unpleasant. However, these events are not a form of punishment or retribution for the "sins" of man. On the one hand, these events are in response to the thoughts of humankind that have accumulated over the millennia. On the other hand, these events are catalysts that will help humankind break through the veil that has held it motionless for so long. Humankind has indeed come to turning points in its history where a decision one way or the other radically altered the timeline of development – either moving it forward significantly or dramatically slowing it down. However, the time you are in now and the events you are about to witness are different from anything that has occurred on your planet. At this moment you are standing on stage and ready to witness the greatest transformation of spirit humankind has ever experienced.

For some of you this transformation will be an effortless process whereby your heart will open (figuratively) and you will see life in a new way – you will be free from hatred, greed and fear. For others the process will take a little more effort on your part – you will have to dig deep into your psyche and try to root out feelings of hatred, greed and fear, but you will do it because these emotions feel alien and destructive and you will know at your core they are not for you and not part of your forward progress. Then there are others among you who will not change one bit, because it is not a part of who you are at this point in your development. For those of you who will not change life will be difficult – even cruel.

However, the hardship and pain will not come about because you are being punished, because you are not. The hardship and pain will come about because that is what you are here to experience at this time. In the larger picture, we all have reasons for doing the things we do, experiencing the things we choose to experience. Some of us are ready to move into the next level of experience and existence but many of us are not, and this is exactly the way it should be. Forgive those who have caused you pain and anguish, regardless of where they are on their path of development, because that is what *your* level of development requires. Do not concern yourself with what another person's level of development requires of him or her.

62

Consciousness

MATTER IS BEING PROJECTED all the time. The question is – into what form is this matter being projected? The "final" form of matter depends on our level of consciousness, because it is our consciousness that directs matter and energy. Our consciousness creates energy and then this energy becomes matter, which is a physical manifestation of our consciousness. This is why we say your perception becomes your reality – your tangible reality. Your perception is directed or created by your consciousness, so everything really begins in and with your consciousness. So, the state of your consciousness determines your inner and outer worlds. By focusing on your consciousness and its development, you can easily change your world and the world around you. You focus on your consciousness when you go within and reconnect with your inner core.

Matter is our reality. There are, of course, other realities but very few of us are actively aware of them at this time. Therefore, if you want to see your current level of consciousness all you need to do is look at your life and the world around you. Is your life happy? Is it peaceful? Are all your needs met without effort? Do you love your neighbor as you love yourself? Do you treat others as you would have them treat you? If you answered "No" to any of these questions, you have some work to do on your consciousness. In this case "consciousness" means your state and level of awareness of what is going on around you and what is going on inside of you. Just because you "think" you are aware does not necessarily make it so.

The mere fact that you are thinking or processing thoughts through your mind tells you that you are at a lower than optimal state of awareness and consciousness. You will see that as your state of awareness and consciousness truly begin to develop and progress you will no longer need to process thoughts through your mind. There will no longer be the same delay in releasing the initial energy of a thought, having a thought and then witnessing the physical manifestation of that energy in the world around you. As you develop into beings of higher consciousness, you will see that the time between the energy of a thought, an actual thought and the physical manifestation of that thought will be infinitesimal. This is what it means to be a being of higher consciousness – you create and change your world in an instant, because you are no longer held down by your current understanding of the laws of physics. You will see the universe as the beautiful and wondrous place it really is. You will no longer be limited by your current understandings, because as your consciousness develops and grows, you will begin to understand the true meaning of the universe and consciousness itself. Consciousness has a purpose, just as your life has a purpose. There is a reason consciousness exists, just as there is a reason why you have access to it.

At this moment in time you have an even greater access to and awareness of consciousness because humankind is at a crossroads. Humankind has the unique opportunity to leapfrog on the scale of human evolutionary development. Humankind has at its disposal numerous methods to help itself move along the development of consciousness.

Consciousness is real. It is not something that is make believe or only for the select few. Consciousness is there to be accessed and enjoyed by all, just as the so-called mysteries of the universe are there to be accessed and known by all.

63

Open Your Heart and
See a New Reality

THERE ARE NO SECRETS in the universe and nothing is intentionally hidden from your view. If you cannot "see" or "perceive" something, it is your fault and not that of the universe or the universal creator. Does this sound harsh? It is not meant to. It is meant to wake you up, help you to open your eyes to the world around you and your role in this world. You are meant to fly free and have the faith and curiosity to explore the world around you and the gifts you have within your spirit – gifts you have been carrying around for lifetimes, but are only now beginning to access. This is the best time to be alive because you are standing on the doorstep of a new reality (again, new for you), a new way of existing. The hard part of getting to this point is over, or just about to be. You have done the work over many lifetimes and now you are ready to collect the reward – now you are ready to walk through that door into a blissful and peaceful existence, where there is harmony amongst people and with nature.

You will no longer be struggling to make ends meet, or trying to understand why your life is the way it is, why your job is so unsatisfying, or why your spouse is so darned obstinate. You will now begin to see that all these situations were created by you and *are* you. Your external world is a reflection of your internal world, and your internal world is but a reflection of the state of your consciousness. You see, it all keeps coming back to your level or state of consciousness. This is a key point. Your level or state of consciousness is what drives the universe. It is your consciousness that originally created the universe, brought it into existence.

You see, your consciousness has been around and has been active a lot longer than you realize. Your consciousness is where it all began eons upon eons ago. Your consciousness is your essence, the eternal part of "you" that has always been and will always be. This essence, this energy, cannot be destroyed. It is this energy that drives forward creation. It is this energy that defines your existence, your state of being. The state of your awareness, the development level of your consciousness, is what determines how you perceive the world – what you "see" and what remains "unseen". Your consciousness acts as your filter by blocking out things you are not ready to see and letting in those things you are ready to see. Life is a process. Just as you are born and develop with age and time, so too your consciousness develops over time (eons rather than years). You are standing at the end of a very long and winding road which all of you have traveled. There is not one person among you who has not been on this road for eons and eons. But you have finally arrived at the point where all your suffering can end. You have finally arrived at the point where you can look up and begin to see the magnificence of yourselves by seeing the magnificence of the universe. You are no different than the most glorious spring day, the most beautifully created snowflake, the most delicately scented flower. You are all these things and more because you created them, or rather your essence, your consciousness, did.

This is what it is time to learn, to realize again, that you are the creator of your world and this universe. There is nothing going on in this universe that you did not have a part in creating. You are the mastermind and you all have the mind of a master, if you will but look within and reconnect with your core being. Acknowledge your power, your creativity and your magnificence by focusing on what is going on inside of *you* and not just what is going on inside your head. Feel your heart; feel your soul. You are trying to tap into your consciousness, and from that point direct the energy out into the world. It may sound difficult but it really is not. This is no longer something that only great sages and masters can accomplish. You too can reach in and reconnect with your core and thereby tap into your consciousness, and use the power and energy of your consciousness to change the world. The more you tap into your consciousness, the more you will see and understand. The more you see and understand, the faster your consciousness will expand and develop.

64

You Are Truth

THE TRUTH IS OUT THERE and is knowable by everyone. To know the truth, though, you do have to do some work and this work involves getting to know yourself. The truth is not on the outside or in the external world, but is to be found in your internal world. You are the Truth because everything that is found outside of you is also found inside of you. There is no difference between you and the cosmos, which means there is no separation between you and the cosmos. The atoms and molecules that make up your physical body are the same atoms and molecules that make up the planets in the universe, and the atmospheres around each of the billions of planets in the cosmos.

There is nothing that is greater or lesser, more important or less important in the universe, because everything is made up of the same building blocks and structures. Things appear "different" because they vibrate at different speeds – but this is only according to your current perception, which is dictated by your current level of consciousness. As your consciousness shifts to a higher level, your understanding of the universe will also shift, because you will see things in a new way, which means your perception of the world will change. Things not visible to you now will become easily visible to you as your consciousness shifts. Truths that seem unknowable to you now will become easily knowable as your consciousness shifts.

These are the truths which have been locked away inside of you for so long and of which you are only now becoming aware. These truths have been with you since the beginning of time (meaning existence and not linear time) and are a fundamental part of you – part of your essence. The time has now come for humankind to rediscover these truths and to build a world, a society, based on these truths.

In the new age, humans will become much more humble and will live more peacefully with nature and all neighbors. The time of controlling one's world through the use of force and violence will end. Corruption and nepotism will end because there will be no need for them. Humanity will work together to solve its problems, instead of working against each other. Another's loss will not be your gain. Another's loss will indeed be your loss, and you will soon see this truth clearly and fully understand it. This is what will change the behavior and outlook for humanity – you will begin to feel and fully understand that you are completely connected to the world around you. You will begin to see and understand that what happens to this molecule over here also happens on some level to that molecule over there. There will be no more disconnection between beings. You are all one – be it with your neighbor, your family, your pet, your front lawn, a tree, a rock, a lobster or a planet!

Said another way, the Universal Consciousness is indeed the consciousness of the universe. Yes, the universe has a consciousness, just as you do. The only difference is that the universe's consciousness is the whole, whereas your consciousness is only part of the whole – or so you believe. The universe's consciousness is not greater than your consciousness, because the universe's consciousness is merely your consciousness on a grander scale. By "grander scale" we mean more developed and highly evolved. The universe's consciousness has already reached its highest level of development. It did not evolve over time. It always has been and always will be fully developed and fully evolved.

The part of your consciousness that humankind is currently accessing is not that highly evolved in the overall picture of what is possible. However, this is about to change for the vast majority of you on Earth at this time. You are so close to the next stage in the evolution of your consciousness. You are about to make a grand leap forward and experience life on a whole new level – a level where you are not disconnected from yourself or others. Once you reconnect with yourself, your inner core, your inner knowledge, you will never want to go back to the level of consciousness where you have been for decades and eons. Once you see and feel what the new life is like, you will want to move forward even faster. You will find the new existence to be very "more-ish", the more you feel, the more you will want to experience. You will no longer be asleep at the wheel, going through life in a semi-comatose state. You will embrace life and all of its experiences with a passion and understanding you have never before experienced. You will be fully aware for the first time in a very long time.

65

Your Purpose Is
Grander than Yourself

THE END IS NOT NEAR, but the beginning is. You have set before you the chance of a lifetime, the chance of many lifetimes actually. You are standing ready to plunge into a new reality, a new way of seeing and perceiving, a new way of existing. From now on, nothing will ever be the same for you. You will see good in all people; you will see good in all situations, because you will be seeing from a different perspective – a perspective that looks at the whole person or situation, instead of only at a part of it. You will begin to have a more complete view and understanding of the world around you and the universe. When you have a more complete view of the universe, you will have a more complete understanding of everything that is in the universe, which also means you will have a more complete understanding of yourself and your purpose for living.

Once you truly understand your purpose for living, you will be reconnected with yourself and the universe and you will be truly happy and content. This is what humanity is moving toward – an understanding of its existence. You will begin to see what you came here to do and how that can be done. Your purpose for living is grander than yourself although for many years now humankind has been limiting its existence to the mere survival of itself. This is what will change. This is what has to change. Humankind is not here merely for itself. Humankind is here for a far greater purpose than its mere existence. Humankind is here to help the universe and the Universal Consciousness expand and move to greater heights of awareness of itself and that which is around it and within it.

The fuller human experience becomes, i.e., the more humans can raise their consciousness and awareness, the greater the experience will be for all forms of consciousness, including the universe's consciousness. The universe's consciousness is there and will always be there. However, the fuller and more aware all the other consciousnesses that make up the universe's consciousness can become, so too can the universe's consciousness thrive and expand even more. It is kind of like having a glass of cloudy, muddy water. It is water but it is not too much fun to look at or drink. However, if you have a glass of crystal pure water it really fires the imagination and happy thoughts, and you want to drink more and more of it. So, do you want a cloudy, muddy consciousness or do you want a crystal clear consciousness?

66

No One Is More Powerful
than You

NATURE HAS A WAY OF POPPING UP when you least expect it and in ways you least expect, just as human nature has a way of acting and reacting in the most surprising of ways. This is what is about to start occurring on a large scale. People will start to behave in ways you thought impossible and inconceivable only a few years ago. Some of these behaviors will surprise you in a good way, while others will surprise you in an unpleasant way. There is nothing you can do about it at this point except to try to go with the flow, and not try to understand why they are doing what they are doing. Why they are doing what they are doing is not your concern, although you will often be affected by what other people do.

Over the next few years it is important to remain true to yourself and your individual beliefs. Do not be led astray by those who pose as your friends but do not have your best interest at heart. If you see someone behaving in a hypocritical or two-faced manner, turn and go the other way. You must learn to practice discernment in what you do and whom you choose to have around you. The time for leniency in friendships is over. This does not mean you should be hateful or fearful of others. It means you must remain true to yourself and what you believe. If those around you do not believe as you believe, just walk away, but do not wish them ill or have negative thoughts about them. Accept them as they are (as you would have them accept you as you are), wish them well and move on.

There will be enough people in the world that think as you think, so you will never be alone. As one door closes, another will open and as one friendship ends another will take its place. But the one that takes its place will be more suited to your beliefs and more in line with your purpose. We are coming to a time when like will attract like, and like will coalesce with like more than ever before. You will soon find that the people and situations you encounter seem tailor-made for you – they will help you progress and develop as a human being and expand your level of consciousness. This is not accidental but part of a grander scheme to help humankind move forward on the evolutionary scale.

You always have help and you are never alone. It is your feeling and fear of disconnection that has turned so many of your lives into a living hell, and created so much violence and greed in your world. By reconnecting with yourself, you will reconnect with the universe and you will begin to see and feel that you are not alone and never were alone. Remember, you always have help but it is found within you and not outside of you. No one is more powerful than you. No one is more brilliant than you. All knowledge and all sources of inspiration and creativity are within you. There is nothing that exists that you do not already possess or share. All is yours – it is just a matter of reconnecting and accessing it.

67

You Are Finally at
the Edge of Paradise

THE END IS NOT NEAR but the future is. Humanity is on the brink of a new beginning, a new future, and a new way of being. The first step has already been taken and now what remains is to take the next few steps into the future – a future that promises all you ever hoped for as a group and more. You are finally here – at the edge of paradise where the world is free from poverty and hatred, from violence and corruption, from self-serving and runaway egos. You are about to enter a new world where your heart's desire will be yours. Your hearts will be full of compassion and unconditional love, because you will once again understand how the universe operates and what is necessary for you to be your true self, not some sort of hybrid – neither completely lacking in compassion nor fully compassionate. In case you were wondering, humankind has never been entirely without compassion. Even in the worst of times and in the worst of situations humankind has at its core compassion and unconditional love, because those are the building blocks from whence all life originated.

In the next few years you will find you are returning more to your essence, your natural state of being. This is by design. Having said this though, nothing in your life is pre-determined. You always have free will and the ability to create any outcome you want. You often have difficulty creating different outcomes, however, because you do not fully understand the laws of the universe and the true relationship between energy, thoughts and matter or physical reality. This is about to change. Many of you will have to study these relationships and relearn them, while others among you will just "wake up" one morning with full knowledge and understanding. Once you again understand the laws of the universe you will say, "How could I ever have forgotten this?" But you have and now the situation is about to change for the better for the majority of you.

The road ahead is neither as long nor as difficult as many would have you believe. Remember to trust in yourself and your completeness. Trust in your ability to see through the tricks and shams people will use to try and deceive you. The next few years will be a bit of a roller coaster ride as the old ways dissolve and the new ways take hold and grow. This is why we keep urging you to go within and find peace by reconnecting with your inner core. As you reconnect with your inner core, knowledge and information – both mystical and practical – will come to you. This will make your life easier and the transition smoother.

68

You Can Perform Miracles

JUST AS THERE IS NOT ONE WAY to reach enlightenment, neither is there one way to reach the next stage of evolution. However, in order to reach the next stage of evolution, each and every one of you will have to regain access or reconnect with your inner core. If you do not do this, you will not be able to move to the next stage, because your system will not be properly aligned with the energies that flow at that state of existence. This is what aligning with your inner core is all about – it prepares you for the energies that "reside" at the next level. Of course, the sooner you reconnect with your inner core and "align" yourself with the new energies, the sooner you will begin to see life anew – from a different perspective – and the sooner you will be able to perform miracles. You were not expecting to perform miracles, were you? They will only seem to be miracles from your current limited perspective. When you are aligned with the new energies, you will have a new understanding of the universe and its laws. Therefore, with this new understanding will come greater power to manipulate and direct energy and matter, in a productive way, to create what you would now consider to be miracles.

The way ahead is clear. There will be some upheavals but overall you will be fine as long as you are working to reconnect with your inner core and inner sense of being. As you begin to shift to the next level of consciousness, you will find your view of the world and the events of the world will begin to shift. What would have crushed you, defeated you, made you inconsolable just a few years or months ago will no longer have the same overwhelming effect on you. You will find that as you watch the news you will feel compassion, but not the same sorrow you once would have felt. Nor will you feel the same anger or jealousy you used to feel. You will find your emotional state will become more balanced, more level and harmonious, regardless of what you experience, see or read about. This is a natural progression as you move closer to a complete shift in consciousness. The hardest step is actually the first step. After you make the initial recognition that you want to reconnect with your inner core, each step becomes faster and easier until you are moving at what could be called light speed.

The way ahead is clear. Your future is clear. Your next move is clear for all who wish to see and acknowledge that we are on the verge of a new beginning, a new state of being, a new form of existence. The next leap in consciousness will not take decades or even years. It can be fully accomplished in a matter of months for those of you who have the wish to reconnect with your inner core. Again, there is no one way to fully reconnect with your inner core. The methods mentioned in this book are only suggestions, but are by no means the only way. Once you make the determination that you want to reconnect with your true self, the method and way will be put before you. You will not be able to miss it – as long as you have made the decision to reconnect with your inner core, you cannot be left behind or miss the boat.

Some people will take months to fully reconnect, while others will take only weeks or even just days. It doesn't matter how long it takes to reconnect, because all of you will get there with time to spare. If it is your intention to reconnect, you cannot fail. This is one of the laws of the universe that has not been part of your psyche in a very long time. Nothing and no one can prevent you from moving forward on the evolutionary scale, including yourself. When the right combination of energies, thoughts and intention are in alignment, the doors will be opened and all you have to do is walk through them. All you have to do is the small amount of work in aligning yourself – that's it – and the rest is pretty much done for you. You have help. You have guidance. You have everything you need. There is nothing in this universe you lack. You are all-powerful. You are magnificent. The time has come for you to start believing in yourself and seeing what you are capable of. You are capable of great joy, great tranquility, great love, and great compassion.

This is not the end, but the beginning.

Exercises

ONE

Reconnect with Your Inner Core

Doing this exercise two or three times a week will help you live within yourself and in alignment with your inner being.

Step 1

Sit quietly in a room without distraction or noise. Listen to your breath and watch it move in and out of your nostrils. Focus on your heart area and just be for about five minutes. See what is there and feel what is there. As your breath rate slows and becomes even and steady you are ready to move on to the second step in this process.

Step 2

With your eyes closed, take an inventory of what you want in life and from life. Think about things that happened years ago and think about things that happened yesterday. Think about things that make you sad and make you happy. Think about things that make you angry and those that make you joyful – just don't stop thinking, not at this point. Feel the emotions rush through your mind and your body. Feel the full weight and impact these emotions have on your system and on your breathing. Once you have done this for several minutes stop all thoughts and just relax with your eyes closed.

Step 3

Now, take your right hand and place it on your left shoulder. Sit for several minutes – thinking of nothing, if possible.

Put your right hand back down on your lap – it does not matter which way the palm is facing.

Pull your shoulders down and back so your spine is tall and straight. Feel the energy that has been released as it crawls up your spine and into your crown chakra. Feel the direct connection with the universe. Feel your inner core begin to open up and connect once again with the Universal Consciousness and all that is out there. Feel your body as it comes alive and shines from within. Breathe in as deeply as possible a few times and then settle back into a regular breathing pattern. Let go of your fears and worries. Let go of anything you feel might be keeping you in this dimension. Let go and feel the freedom it brings. Let your mind and body wander into the depths of your soul previously closed off to you and your senses. Let go and breathe in the air of freedom and possibility.

TWO

Ground

This exercise will help you understand why you are here and how you can help humanity move to the next level of consciousness.

Start this exercise by being alone and at one with your heartbeat. Listen to your heartbeat and focus only on that for 5-10 minutes each day. As you do this you are grounding yourself and aligning your heartbeat with that of the Earth's.

THREE

Live in the Present

This exercise will keep you grounded in the here and now and will help you see/perceive reality as it is.

The joy of living is being in the present, without concerns about the future. To live life to the fullest one must be in contact with one's inner being. Being in contact with one's inner being merely means being in contact with one's inner core by being aware of the life force that runs through each of us. We accomplish this by being aware of the present and what is occurring around us.

To be fully present, look around you and notice what is there. Is there a table, a lamp, a child, or a pet? Whatever is around you is the present. Don't let your mind wander to events of the day, or jump to the past or future. Be fully in the now.

Several times a day, look around and really see what is there. This is how to live in the present. This grounds you in the here and now.

FOUR

Activate the Energy of Unconditional Love

This is a one-off exercise that will activate the energy of unconditional love in you and help humanity make the leap to the next level of consciousness.

This energy is available to everyone.

Once this energy has been activated within your energy system and your consciousness, you will begin to see a difference in the world around you. This energy has not been present in your consciousness to this extent for a very long time. The time has now come for unconditional love to reassert itself in your consciousness, so that humanity may, as a group, evolve to the next higher stage of being.

Step 1
Fully imagine the feeling of true, unconditional love. Immerse yourself in unconditional love.

Step 2
As this feeling washes over you, pull it deep into your solar plexus and hold it there for a few minutes.

Step 3
Slowly release unconditional love back into the universe.

FIVE

Weigh Your Decisions

This exercise will assist you in making the best* choice possible.

Step 1
Relax and ground yourself by taking a few deep breaths, making sure to exhale long and full.

Step 2
State your decision and ask your higher self if this choice feels right.

Step 3
If your stated decision is the right* one for you at this moment, you will feel a lightness in your solar plexus.

If your stated decision is the wrong* one for you at this time you will feel a heaviness in your solar plexus.

* There are no "right" or "wrong" choices in life. Please see Chapter 20 "Every Decision is Perfect" for further explanation.

CPSIA information can be obtained at www.ICGtesting.com
Printed in the USA
LVOW030624281211

261336LV00002B/8/P